Law and Society
Recent Scholarship

Edited by Melvin I. Urofsky

A Series from LFB Scholarly

Legal Intellectual Movements in Political Time

Reconstructive Leadership and Transformations of Legal Thought and Discourse

Simon Zschirnt

LFB Scholarly Publishing LLC
El Paso 2015

Library of Congress Cataloging-in-Publication Data

Zschirnt, Simon, 1979- author.
Legal intellectual movements in political time : reconstructive leadership and transformations of legal thought and discourse / Simon Zschirnt.
pages cm
Based on author's thesis (doctoral - Washington State University, School of Politics, Philosophy & Public Affairs, 2013) issued under title: The political foundations of legal theory : political realignment and the legal marketplace of ideas.
Includes bibliographical references and index.
ISBN 978-1-59332-800-9 (hardcover : alk. paper)
1. Law--Political aspects--United States. 2. United States--Politics and government. 3. Law--United States--Philosophy. I. Title.
KF380.Z73 2015
349.73--dc23
2015021414

ISBN 978-1-59332-800-9

Manufactured in the United States of America.

Table of Contents

List of Figures

List of Tables

CHAPTER 1

The Cycles of Political and Legal Time

INTRODUCTION

"People don't understand what the law schools were like 20 years ago" explains Gary Lawson, one of the founding members of the Federalist Society, the nation's leading conservative legal professional organization. "[A]nyone who said anything out of the orthodoxy would get hissed."[1] Although the liberal orthodoxy that Lawson is referring to retains a strong presence in the law schools, conservative approaches to the law have since enjoyed a remarkable resurgence in the legal marketplace of ideas, one that has paralleled conservative trends in national politics. This phenomenon and its historical antecedents are the subject of this book, which examines the dynamics of the relationship between changes in electoral politics and changes in legal thought. In particular, it examines the reasons for the congruence between the cycle of conservative and liberal trends in national politics and the cycle of formalist and instrumentalist trends in legal thought. Its thesis is that this congruence is not merely coincidental or the product of the independent action of historical forces upon electoral politics and the legal profession. Instead, it is in large part the result of political change facilitating change in the legal profession by legitimating new approaches to the law. This proposition is tested by examining the temporal relationship between the three most recent realignments of the political system and their associated changes in constitutional discourse, constitutional jurisprudence, and legal education and pedagogy. This analysis finds that the legal profession is generally responsive to realities of power and that the embrace of new approaches to the law by political actors during periods of political realignment can have a legitimating effect. However, the importance of this effect in changing the climate of the legal marketplace of ideas is contingent upon the comprehensiveness of the realignment and upon the degree to which a new approach to the law has an existing foothold in the legal marketplace of ideas.

LAW, JUDICIAL EMPOWERMENT, AND THE POLITICAL REGIME

Models of legal change that identify electoral politics, specifically realignments of the political system that replace one political-electoral regime with another, as a key to understanding the evolution of legal thought and jurisprudence have been widely accepted. The seminal work in this line of scholarship has been Dahl's classic study, which observed that "the Supreme Court is inevitably a part of the dominant national alliance."[2] Dahl's argument that trends in jurisprudence on the Court have inevitably followed trends in electoral politics turned the conventional wisdom of its time regarding judicial review on its head. In particular, legal scholars had theretofore struggled with the legitimacy of un-elected judges nullifying the work of the people's elected representatives. This struggle became particularly acute in the decades following the confrontation between President Franklin Roosevelt and the Court over the constitutionality of the New Deal. The ambivalence toward judicial review that this episode engendered was reflected in the tone of legal scholarship during this period, most notably Bickel's *The Least Dangerous Branch*, which argues that "judicial review is a deviant institution in the American democracy" and coined the phrase "counter-majoritarian difficulty."[3]

Dahl's analysis demonstrating that most exercises of the power of judicial review have in fact furthered the dominant national political coalition's policy agenda by expunging policies enacted by the previous regime fundamentally changed the terms of the debate surrounding judicial review. Contextualizing Roosevelt's struggle against the Court as a historical aberration, it demonstrated that the Court is best understood as a majoritarian rather than a counter-majoritarian institution. The reason for this is the political nature of the selection process for federal judges, who are usually drawn by presidents from the ranks of party loyalists and ideological allies with an eye toward achieving particular policy goals.[4] Given the regularity of vacancies on the Court, this partisan method of selection ensures that the constitutional values that hold sway on the Court will not be in conflict with those that hold sway in the elected branches of government for any extended period of time.

Integral to this understanding of the Supreme Court in the context of regime politics is Skowronek's concept of "political time," which refers to the life cycle of political-electoral regimes.[5] As Skowronek illustrates, the dynamics of presidential leadership are contingent upon the president's place in political time. In particular, they are contingent upon whether the president is affiliated with or opposed to the dominant national political coalition and its values, with presidents falling into one of four categories: reconstructive presidents, articulation presidents, preemptive presidents, and disjunctive presidents. Reconstructive presidents are presidents who govern during periods of political realignment and lead the construction of new regimes. According to Skowronek's typology these include presidents such as Abraham Lincoln, Franklin Roosevelt, and Ronald Reagan. Following in the footsteps of reconstructive presidents are articulation presidents, presidents who are affiliated with a regime and its values during periods in which the regime remains dominant. These include presidents such as Theodore Roosevelt, Harry Truman, and George H.W. Bush. The most common type of president, these presidents are generally "orthodox innovators," leaders who successfully adapt the regime's values to new circumstances and manage divisions within their political coalitions.[6] Members of the opposition party who are opposed to the regime and its values yet manage to capture the presidency during periods in which the regime remains dominant are preemptive presidents. These include presidents such as Woodrow Wilson, Dwight Eisenhower, and Bill Clinton. Often elected as a result of divisions within the dominant national political coalition, these presidents are constrained in their ability to effect significant change and their political successes are typically limited to moderating the regime's more extreme tendencies. Finally, disjunctive presidents are presidents who are affiliated with a regime and its values but govern during periods in which the regime is in decline and the political system is in flux. These include presidents such as James Buchanan, Herbert Hoover, and Jimmy Carter. Presiding over regimes that have been rendered vulnerable by national crises, these presidents' efforts to respond to these crises by pressing major departures from their regimes' orthodoxies have inevitably been doomed to failure and have hastened the demises of these regimes.

A president's place in political time not only shapes their general ability to lead and to implement their political agenda, it also shapes their relationship with the courts. Reconstructive presidents leading the construction of new regimes have generally had contentious relationships with Supreme Courts that have been staffed by presidents affiliated with the previous regime and that are committed to the previous regime's values. This has often taken the form of efforts to curb judicial independence and anti-judicial rhetoric in which judges serve as "politically isolated…representative[s] of the old, discredited commitments and entrenched interests" and useful "foil[s] to enhance the president's own authority."[7] However, periods of reconstruction are usually relatively brief and in normal times the relationship between the Court and the elected branches of government has generally been a harmonious one. Once a regime has entrenched its legal ideology on the bench, presidents who are affiliated with the regime have found the Court to be a useful ally in implementing regime policies. Moreover, even preemptive presidents who are opposed to the regime and may disagree with the Court's understandings of the law have had better relations with the Court than might be anticipated. Not only have such presidents usually been moderates who share many of the regime's values despite their partisan affiliations, they have often relied upon the Court to protect their institutional prerogatives in partisan conflicts with Congress.

Law and courts scholars who have adopted a "political regimes" approach have subsequently refined these observations through a large body of research. In particular, they have illustrated in greater detail the entrenchment of regimes' constitutional visions through the judicial appointment process as well as the collaborative role played by the courts in the implementation of regimes' policy agendas. For example, it has been shown that trends in the Court's criminal justice jurisprudence can best be explained in terms of broad trends in electoral politics, specifically the increasing politicization of crime and its role in the disintegration of the New Deal regime and the construction of the New Right regime, rather than in terms of the individual constitutional and political values of its justices.[8] While the members of the Court appointed prior to the election of 1968 shared a liberal approach to criminal procedure cases that transcended partisanship, sharp partisan cleavages began to emerge on the Court in the early 1970s. This change coincided with crime control policy emerging as a major political issue and the New Right regime following through on campaign promises to move the Court's criminal justice jurisprudence in a more conservative direction. These cleavages were the result of a distinctive cohort of Republican appointees joining the Court who, despite disagreeing on other issues, were appointed in large part as a result of their conservative views on criminal procedure. Similar patterns are also evident in the Court's jurisprudence in other areas that have been of particular interest to the leadership of the New Right regime and have played a particularly important role in decisions by Republican presidents regarding judicial selection, such as federalism.[9]

While changes in jurisprudence have been driven by the rise of new political-electoral regimes whose judicial appointees bring distinctive constitutional visions to the courts, these visions are not entirely exogenous. Instead, these constitutional visions are to a significant extent shaped and constrained by inherited institutional dynamics. For example, the unprecedented activism of the Rehnquist Court was a product of the intercurrence of the rights-based constitutionalism of the Warren Court, which permanently transformed the role of the Supreme Court in the American political system and the norms surrounding the Court's use of judicial power, and the New Right regime's critiques of legal liberalism and the welfare state.[10] While conservative attacks on the Warren Court had traditionally focused upon the Court's activism, which they characterized as undemocratic and illegitimate, once Republican control of the presidency had given the Court a Republican majority, that majority would not lead the Court toward a renewed commitment to judicial restraint. Instead, inheriting an institution that had been transformed into a forum for vindicating individual rights claims, it would build upon the Warren Court's "institutionalization of judicial activism" by enforcing its own distinctively conservative form of rights-based constitutionalism.[11]

This constitutional vision has been reflected in several lines of precedent that have demonstrated that an activist judiciary can serve conservative ends as well as liberal ends. Not only has the Court aggressively attempted to roll back the post-New Deal expansion of the federal government generally by resurrecting the Interstate Commerce Clause and 10th and 11th Amendments as judicially enforceable limitations on congressional power, it has also aggressively attempted to roll back the expansion of the administrative state specifically by resurrecting the non-delegation doctrine. It has also recognized a host of new individual rights with a conservative tenor in cases involving issues such as affirmative action, property rights, and the rights of religious groups to equal access to government resources. Although parallels between the Warren Court and the Burger and Rehnquist Courts have been rejected by most conservatives, who argue that conservative judicial activism is "fundamentally different from the sort of judicial activism long favored by liberal interest groups" because it seeks to "defend individual rights against intrusive or overbearing governmental activity" rather than initiate "programs of social reform," both styles of jurisprudence share a willingness to challenge longstanding precedent and legislative and administrative practice.[12]

It is not only jurisprudence but also attitudes toward judicial power that have been politically constructed by changes in the political-electoral regime. In particular, the ebbs and flows of the debate between the proponents of departmentalism and the proponents of judicial supremacy have also largely corresponded to the cycle of political time.[13] Departmentalist arguments advocating independent interpretation of the Constitution by each branch of government have become prominent in constitutional discourse during periods of realignment. During these periods the constitutional values of the judiciary are likely to be incongruent with those of Congress and the president and departmentalism provides a pretense for promoting the new regime's constitutional vision. Conversely, judicial supremacist arguments advocating that the Supreme Court be the ultimate interpreter of the Constitution have become prominent in constitutional discourse during periods in which the political system is stable. During these periods the constitutional values of the judiciary are likely to be congruent with those of Congress and the president and bolstering judicial authority is in the regime's interest. In particular, promoting judicial supremacy serves a "regime maintenance" function, reinforcing the ability of the Court to enforce the constitutional values of the regime against resisters at the state and local levels whom federalism places beyond the direct control of Congress and the president. It also provides a form of insurance against "failure[s] of will" by political actors affiliated with the regime who may deviate from these constitutional values as a result of short-term political calculations.[14]

The promotion of judicial supremacy has also allowed political actors to avoid taking ownership of divisive issues, such as slavery, civil rights, and abortion, which can fracture regimes.[15] For example, although the Court's decision in *Dred Scott v. Sandford* has been widely criticized as a "self-inflicted wound" caused by an activist Court intent upon imposing its views on slavery upon the nation, these criticisms misread the case's historical context.[16] In fact, the case was pushed upon the Court by a Congress and a president who were eager to rid themselves of the troublesome slavery issue. Not only did the case reach the Court as a result of legislation fast-tracking Supreme Court review of cases involving slavery, the Court was publicly encouraged to provide a final and definitive resolution of the issue by President James Buchanan and by other leading figures in both major political parties, who consistently framed the slavery issue as a "judicial question which legitimately belongs to the Supreme Court of the United States."[17] The promotion of judicial supremacy by national political leaders has taken the form not only of this type of rhetorical support for judicial power but also of deliberately ambiguous statutes drafted in an effort to respond to public demand for legislative action on important national issues without alienating important constituencies. Such statutes, most prominently the Sherman Anti-Trust Act, have succeeded on several occasions in deflecting responsibility for whatever policy ultimately emerges onto the courts. The purposeful transformation of divisive issues from political issues into legal issues has thus allowed regimes to effectively manage divisions within their ranks.

That judicial empowerment is best understood in the context of regime maintenance is illustrated not only by historical patterns of rhetorical support for judicial supremacy but also by the institutional evolution of the federal judiciary. As Gillman illustrates, prior to the Civil War the federal judiciary was a much smaller and weaker institution than it is today, one whose judges were "overworked, poorly paid, and authorized to enforce only a subset of federal law."[18] It was not until the subsequent reorganization of federal judicial circuits, addition of federal judgeships, and expansion of federal court jurisdiction that occurred between the 1870s and the 1890s that the federal judiciary began to assume its modern significance in the American political system. This empowerment of the federal judiciary represented a strategic decision on the part of the Republican regime of the 3rd Party System that was intended to nationalize the laissez faire economic policies that it favored by increasing federal supervision of state and local economic regulations. Entrenching the regime's economic values in the judiciary served to protect these values against the tenuousness of Republican control of Congress and the presidency during this period at a time when there was growing populist backlash against the regime's economic conservatism.

Judicial empowerment has also been found to rest upon political foundations in the international context. As Hirschl argues, the global trend toward powerful constitutional courts and entrenched rights guarantees can be understood as a rearguard effort at "hegemonic preservation" on the part of economic and political elites concerned with insulating neo-liberal policies from popular pressure.[19] For example, Israel's transition from a state with a strong tradition of parliamentary sovereignty to one with an activist constitutional court that has been quite willing to use its power of judicial review can be understood as an effort by the country's traditional secular elite to preempt the rising political influence of the country's growing Orthodox Jewish population by constitutionalizing issues relating to the role of religion in public life. Similarly, the entrenchment of the Canadian Charter of Rights and Freedoms, particularly its provisions relating to language rights, can be understood as an effort by Canada's leaders to preempt the rising political influence of Quebecois nationalists by transferring the issue of Quebec's status as a distinct francophone society from the political arena to the courts. In these and other cases, judicial empowerment has been promoted by traditional elites as a way of transferring decision-making authority from political arenas where those elites' hegemony is under threat to the courts, which are believed to be more firmly in elites' grasp.

Although regimes have often been conceptualized as existing during discrete historical periods characterized by dominant national political coalitions associated with particular political parties, values, and policies, it is important to note the degree to which the concept of a regime is fluid. As Carmines and Stimson illustrate, realignments of the political system do not occur through abrupt transitions from one party system to another but rather through a gradual process of issue evolution.[20] The first stage of this four-stage process involves political elites framing an issue or cluster of related issues in partisan terms, usually for electoral advantage. Taking its cue from political elites, the mass public then changes its perception of the parties with regard to those issues. This change in perception in turn changes voters' affect toward the parties, destabilizing existing partisan affiliations. The result is partisan polarization that corresponds to the line of cleavage created by the new issues. Most importantly, this process is not limited to discrete periods of realignment but rather is continuous, as the political system is constantly evolving in response to the reframing of issues by political elites. Moreover, as Orren and Skowronek illustrate, not only are regimes characterized by considerable dynamism, their constituent elements and policies often embody multiple and sometimes conflicting political traditions, a phenomenon that Orren and Skowronek term "intercurrence."[21] For example, the New Right regime has been called a "marriage of convenience between populists and economic conservatives," two groups embodying distinctive political traditions that were initially brought together by their shared "opposition to the federal government as sponsor of the social change catalyzed by the movements for civil rights, women's rights, consumer rights, and the environment" but which have increasingly parted ways on issues such as gay rights, immigration, and stem cell research.[22] Thus, "any realistic description of politics in time will include multiple orders."[23]

THE ROLE OF SUPPORT STRUCTURES FOR LEGAL CHANGE

While it is clear that changes in jurisprudence have been closely intertwined with political realignments and that the courts represent an integral part of the political-electoral regime, the conditions under which regimes can use the courts to effectively advance their constitutional visions have been the subject of debate. In particular, given the autonomy of the legal profession and, consequently, the autonomy of the courts, it is questionable whether political change is always a sufficient condition for legal change. As case studies of this relationship illustrate, demand-side change in the form of change in the politics of those controlling the judicial appointment process has by itself been insufficient to produce change in judicial outputs absent the creation of a sufficient support structure for legal change within the legal profession.[24] A critical component of such a support structure is the presence of legal entrepreneurs committed to the regime's constitutional vision and capable of providing a sufficient supply of appropriate and properly presented cases.

As Epp's comparative analysis of the interplay of legal entrepreneurs, supreme courts, and civil rights and civil liberties jurisprudence in four countries shows, supreme courts sympathetic to rights claims have found that they can do relatively little to advance rights without organized support for rights litigation that allows rights advocates to effectively pursue their claims in the courts. This requires the presence of "rights advocacy organizations, government-provided legal aid, statutes authorizing the award of attorneys' fees to successful rights plaintiffs, and the...diversification of the legal profession."[25] Without such support from the legal profession and from government, efforts by supreme courts to affect legal change are likely to be "intermittent and ineffective."[26] Thus, for example, although the Supreme Court of India, with the implicit support of the country's political leaders, has consistently indicated its willingness to take an activist approach to individual rights, its landmark rights decisions have remained isolated precedents with little societal impact. This is in large part a reflection of the underdeveloped nature of the Indian legal profession, which has few large law firms (and virtually none of the sort of specialized rights advocacy organizations needed to mount sustained litigation campaigns), an underfunded system of legal aid, and lacks diversity. In contrast, despite the United Kingdom's lack of an entrenched bill of rights and despite the fact that its highest court, the Appellate Committee of the House of Lords, has historically been a conservative institution committed to judicial restraint, a modest "rights revolution" has been achieved thanks to a legal profession whose institutional dynamics have allowed it to force rights issues onto the courts' agenda.

An even more important component of legal change than a legal profession that is able to support legal mobilization is the ability of a new regime's legal ideology to penetrate the legal marketplace of ideas. In particular, the ability of new legal ideologies to achieve acceptance in the legal marketplace of ideas is limited by the fact that the legal profession is a profession governed by strong disciplining norms that limit the scope of argument. As a result, "for legal ideas to be taken seriously by the courts they cannot be seen as wholly novel or outside the realm of legitimate professional opinion."[27] Thus, because the composition of the institutions, such as the legal academy and legal professional organizations, that determine what is and what is not viewed as a serious legal argument is, unlike the staffing of the judiciary, insulated from electoral politics, there is reason to expect that the evolution of legal thought and jurisprudence would also be relatively insulated from the cycle of political time.

Such a disconnect existed during the years following the displacement of the New Deal regime by the New Right regime. Despite the fact that the Republican Party dominated presidential elections after 1968, it initially failed to translate the control of the judicial appointment process that its political ascendancy had produced into a more conservative jurisprudence. Although Republican appointees comprised a majority of the Supreme Court's membership as early as 1972, the Court's jurisprudence in numerous areas of the law continued to disappoint conservatives for many years thereafter. A major reason for this was that the legal profession from which these appointees were drawn continued to be a strongly liberal institution. In particular, public interest litigation continued to be dominated by left-leaning organizations, limiting conservatives' ability to set the courts' agenda and placing them in a perpetually reactive posture. More importantly, the orthodoxies of legal liberalism continued to be the conventional wisdom in the legal academy and legal professional organizations, preventing conservative approaches to the law from gaining credibility and respectability. Consequently, the fact that a judicial nominee was a Republican was no guarantee that that nominee would implement the New Right regime's legal agenda as a judge.

Indeed, broad surveys of the evolution of American legal thought suggest that this may represent a general pattern in which legal orthodoxy is initially a lagging indicator of political orthodoxy due to the insularity of the legal profession generally and the legal academy in particular.[28] For example, the New Right regime's struggle to legitimate its legal ideology in the face of a legal profession whose values and norms were diametrically opposed to this ideology was a reprise of the earlier struggle of the New Deal regime to legitimate its own legal ideology in the face of similar resistance from the legal profession. Just as the American Bar Association, which conservatives have accused of political bias in its ratings of judicial nominees and which has filed amicus curiae briefs in the Supreme Court in support of a variety of liberal causes such as abortion rights, affirmative action, and gay rights, has been a consistent foe of the New Right regime's legal agenda, the organized legal profession played a similar role during the early years of the New Deal regime. Not only was the American Bar Association then a conservative organization that was a vocal opponent of the New Deal, which its president William Ransom referred to as a "blue print borrowed from old world dictatorship," it consistently opposed the New Deal regime's efforts to promote its vision of a "living" Constitution.[29] Its leaders were therefore dismayed when this vision began to influence constitutional jurisprudence, with one of Ransom's successors publicly declaring that there was a "conviction held by...many...lawyers that the 'Supreme Law of the Land' has been distorted out of its original pattern" by a Supreme Court that had abandoned fidelity to the Constitution under political pressure.[30]

THE SYNCHRONICITY OF POLITICAL AND LEGAL TIME

As political-electoral regimes have consolidated, this type of initial resistance within the legal epistemic community to the legal ideologies associated with them has invariably given way to acceptance. Thus, although each was initially characterized by some level of conflict between political actors and the legal profession, the three most recent realignments of the political system have been closely associated with realignments in legal thought. In each case, understandings of the law that were once considered outside of the mainstream eventually gained acceptance in the legal profession and came to define the mainstream. This has been reflected in trends in legal scholarship and jurisprudence, in the orientation of legal professional organizations, and in the public image of the legal profession generally. Most importantly, the newfound prominence of these once marginalized understandings of the law can in each case be attributed not only to the same social forces that have drove the realignment that was unfolding but also to their explicit embrace by political actors affiliated with the new regime. In particular, the embrace of legal ideologies that dovetail with a regime's policy objectives has served as a means of legitimating those ideologies in the legal marketplace of ideas and thereby exerting indirect influence upon judicial outputs.

The first of these realignments of the legal marketplace of ideas that will be examined in this book corresponded to the transition from the 3rd Party System to the 4th Party System in the late 19th century. This transition saw the political alignments that had been shaped decades earlier by the Civil War and Reconstruction superseded by the rise of new issues brought to the fore by rapid industrialization and urbanization. Whereas issues such as federalism and civil rights had defined the previous political system, these issues became less relevant after the end of Reconstruction. As a result, the Democratic and Republican parties had gradually evolved into vehicles for political patronage that had few substantive differences on matters of policy. It was the parties' responses to the economic downturn of the 1890s and the labor strife and agrarian protest movements that it spawned that would reinvigorate partisan competition. While the Democratic Party adopted a populist platform that embraced the demands of organized labor and farmers, calling for an end to the gold standard and for stricter enforcement of anti-trust laws and regulation of railroads, the Republican Party positioned itself as a conservative bulwark against the threat of socialism. When the Democrats' attempt to regain majority status by constructing a "coalition of…the 'toiling masses'" failed, their association with ideas that were considered radical and harmful to the economic prosperity that the nation was once again enjoying marginalized the party.[31] While the latter years of the 3rd Party System had seen a series of closely contested presidential elections and seen control of Congress regularly alternate between the parties, the election of 1896 tipped the partisan balance decisively in the Republicans' favor. Although the Republican Party continued to dominate national politics as it had during the 3rd Party System, its coalition was broadened and its hold upon Congress and the presidency strengthened by the emergence of these new partisan cleavages.[32]

This realignment of the political system was accompanied by revolutionary change in the predominant conception of the nature of law and the judicial process, change that reinforced the political victory of the forces of economic conservatism. While 19th century legal thought had generally taken an instrumentalist view of the law that conceptualized law as malleable and indeterminate and the role of the judge as a pragmatic policymaker, this conception began to fall out of favor in elite circles in the late 19th century.[33] What took its place was a formalist view of the law that conceptualized law as a complete, autonomous, and apolitical system of rules and principles and the role of the judge as a discoverer rather than a maker of law.[34] This revolution in legal thought was driven by an underlying desire among legal scholars and practitioners to separate law and politics and, more specifically, to separate private law from public law in order to create an independent realm of private rights governed by the application of neutral principles and categorizations rather than by value-laden policy considerations.[35] This idea was put into practice in the line of precedent that is most closely identified with this period, the line of precedent that recognized the "liberty of contract" as a constitutional right. Holding that the state is limited in its power to regulate private contractual relations, this line of precedent nullified a broad range of legislation including minimum wage laws and restrictions on working hours and conditions. Such conceptions of law as a wall between state and society were congruent with the ideology and agenda of the Republican regime that dominated national politics, whose leadership for most of this period was strongly opposed to redistributive or market regulative policies that would disturb this separation.[36]

The second of these realignments saw the 4th Party System and its convergence of political and legal conservatism come to an end the same way that it began, with a national economic crisis that realigned the political system. Just as the Democratic Party had responded to the economic downturn of the 1890s by abandoning its previous commitments to laissez faire economic policies and states' rights and moving in a populist direction, the Democratic Party would respond to the Great Depression by positioning itself as the party of national action. While this had resulted in a decisive defeat in 1896, in 1932 this proved to be the basis for the enduring Democratic majority of the New Deal regime. Previously a largely regional party whose only reliable base of support was in the South, the Democratic Party quickly transformed itself into a national majority party by adding to its Southern base the support of the urban and rural working class and of ethnic, racial, and religious minorities. What united these socially and ideologically disparate constituencies was support for the New Deal's unprecedented expansion of federal regulation of the nation's economy and financial system and of federal efforts to promote social welfare. This revolutionization of the role of government would not only have significant political ramifications but also significant legal ramifications insofar as it challenged inherited understandings of the scope of federal regulatory power under the Constitution. This challenge led to a protracted conflict between the New Deal regime and a Supreme Court still comprised largely of holdovers from the deposed Republican regime of the 4th Party System, a Court that was quite willing to use its power of judicial review to enforce these understandings.

While the Court's eventual acquiescence in the New Deal has generally been understood as a response to the political pressure brought to bear upon the Court by the threat of Franklin Roosevelt's proposed "court packing" plan, it was also consistent with change in the predominant conception of the nature of law and the judicial process. In particular, the formalist view of the law that was prevalent during the 4th Party System was increasingly falling out of favor in the legal academy and profession. Taking its place was a more instrumentalist view of the law that harkened back to the pragmatism of 19th century legal thought. This trend toward instrumentalism was epitomized by the rise of the legal realist movement, which gained prominence at several elite law schools in the 1930s.[37] Legal realism's conception of law as indeterminate and the judicial process as fundamentally political, as well as its consequent skepticism toward formalist distinctions between the public and private spheres and toward claims of fundamental individual rights against the state were wholly congruent with the New Deal regime's project of creating a more powerful regulatory and administrative state.[38] The spirit of legal realism was reflected in a Supreme Court that abandoned formalist understandings of the Constitution that were based upon the original intent of its framers and upon technical distinctions between terms such commerce and manufacturing. It was also reflected in the Court's general posture of deference to Congress and the president, which avoided the substitution of the Court's own political judgments, which realists argued are inherent in the judicial process, for the political judgments of the elected branches of government.[39]

The Court's eventual abandonment of this judicial restraint would play a major role in the third of these realignments, which saw the end of the New Deal regime and its replacement by the New Right regime. As new issues, such as civil rights, crime, and women's rights, rose to prominence, the New Deal regime began to fracture along regional and cultural lines. The passage of the Civil Rights Act of 1964 led to the loss of the once monolithic support that the Democratic Party had enjoyed among Southern whites and the party's adoption of liberal stances on a host of social issues and association with the "counterculture" of the 1960s led to a similar erosion of the party's support among socially conservative whites in the North. The collapse of the New Deal regime was also hastened by the unprecedented activism of the Warren Court. Not only did the Court's decisions expanding the rights of criminal defendants have particular political salience in a time of rising crime rates and urban rioting, the Court's establishment clause decisions erecting a more rigid wall of separation between church and state did much to further alienate traditionalists from the New Deal regime. These fissures in the New Deal coalition were actively exploited by the Republican Party, with Richard Nixon's "Southern strategy" targeting Southern whites disaffected with the Democratic Party and Republican leaders co-opting the mobilization of conservative Christians. While Republicans were able to capitalize upon the collapse of the New Deal coalition, the realignment of the political system that ensued was more partial and protracted than the previous two. On the one hand, the Republican Party dominated presidential elections after 1968. Moreover, the liberal consensus of the New Deal regime collapsed as conservative ideas such as punitive crime control policies, deregulation, and supply-side economics increasingly gained traction in the political marketplace of ideas.[40] However, on the other hand, there was no critical election giving Republicans control of both Congress and the presidency and the realignment of the electorate unfolded over the course of several decades.

Nonetheless, the conservative backlash against the liberalism of the late New Deal regime has been reflected in the legal marketplace of ideas no less than in the political marketplace of ideas. This has taken the form of an originalist countermovement against the style of jurisprudence popularized by the Warren Court, which discarded precedents grounded in the original meaning of the Constitution in favor of precedents grounded in sociological analysis. While originalism as articulated by its more dogmatic proponents such as Robert Bork and Raoul Berger has failed to reach the paradigmatic status in the legal marketplace of ideas previously enjoyed by legal formalism and legal realism, originalism writ large has nonetheless come to permeate constitutional discourse.[41] As Fleming notes, there has been widespread renewed interest in history as a source of constitutional meaning and even those scholars generally identified as the strongest critics of the more doctrinaire forms of originalism have increasingly felt compelled to frame their arguments in originalist terms.[42] Perhaps most importantly, this renewed interest in history as a source of constitutional meaning has migrated to the Supreme Court, with the focus of argumentation for both the Court's liberal and conservative justices increasingly turning to the original intent of the Constitution's framers.[43] Originalism's rise from an approach to constitutional interpretation that appeared to have been relegated to the dustbin of history after the New Deal to a near universal starting point for constitutional dialogue has been closely coupled with the New Right regime's consolidation of its power over American electoral institutions. This is significant insofar as originalist jurisprudence is wholly congruent with the New Right regime's policy agenda. In particular, despite the presence of disparate economic and social conservative elements within the New Right coalition, scholars of the New Right have pointed to originalism as a unifying principle. Specifically, it has been noted that an originalist jurisprudence would further the aims of economic conservatives by limiting the size and regulatory power of the federal government as well as reverse a host of decisions opposed by social conservatives in the areas of the criminal procedure, privacy, and religion.[44]

EXPLANATIONS FOR THE CORRELATION BETWEEN POLITICAL AND LEGAL CHANGE

Although the evolution of legal thought has been closely coupled with realignments of the political system, the causal order of political and legal change has been the subject of debate. Scholarship that has explicitly linked this evolution to politics has generally concluded that political and legal change are independent products of particular historical zeitgeists, be they the classical liberal ethos of the late 19th century, the reformist impulses of the New Deal and Great Society eras, or the conservative backlash of the late 20th century.[45] However, others, such as Teles, have countered that change in legal thought does not necessarily accompany political change absent structural change within the legal profession, change that is relatively idiosyncratic. For example, as Teles illustrates, the rise of the New Deal regime had only a limited impact upon a legal profession that would remain anachronistically conservative in its composition, orientation, and orthodoxies until the expanded availability of legal education produced a more socioeconomically diverse and liberal cohort of lawyers and legal scholars and the public interest law firm emerged as a new and decidedly left-leaning mode of legal mobilization. It was these factors, which were largely independent of electoral politics, which transformed the legal profession from a conservative force into a liberal force.

However, there is reason to believe that changes in political orthodoxy directly facilitate changes in legal orthodoxy given the internal dynamics of the legal profession. The legal profession, as has been frequently noted, is responsive to realities of power and the embrace of ideas relating to the law by those in positions of institutional authority has frequently served to legitimate otherwise marginalized or discredited ideas.[46] Therefore, the expected temporal relationship between political change and legal change is one in which political realignment precedes and subsequently facilitates realignment of the legal marketplace of ideas as the newfound association of legal ideologies with prominent political actors causes those ideologies to gain broader acceptance within the legal profession generally and the legal academy in particular. Although scholars such as Balkin and Levinson have suggested as much, noting that revolutions in legal thought and jurisprudence have been facilitated by the "takeover of those institutions charged with teaching the young by newcomers…inclined to dismiss…the purported verities of their predecessors," they do not elaborate upon why or how this process occurs.[47]

OBJECTIVES AND THE PLAN OF THIS BOOK

In order to fill this gap in our understanding of the relationship between political change and legal change, this book examines the dynamics of change in the legal marketplace of ideas during the three aforementioned periods of political realignment. The timing and magnitude of the changes in legal orthodoxy that occurred during each of these periods was measured using multiple methods. The first of these methods was quantitative analysis of patterns in legal scholarship during each period that measures the extent to which changes in the amount of scholarship embracing (as well as attacking) legal ideologies associated with new regimes correspond to critical events signaling support for those ideologies by prominent political actors affiliated with these regimes. As elite institutions and their associated publications exert a "disproportionate influence on the character of scholarship [and] establish the legal conventional wisdom," the analysis was limited to the most prestigious and influential publications.[48]

The selection of the publications analyzed for each case study was based upon law reviews' citation impacts, as these have been demonstrated to be reflective not only of general influence but also to be highly correlated with institutional prestige.[49] Given the exponential increase in the number of law reviews over the course of the 20th century that saw this number rise from seven in 1900 to 33 in 1930 to 180 in 1980, the number of law reviews examined varied so as to be roughly proportional to the number of law reviews in print during each period under examination.[50] Specifically, subsets of varying sizes of the 15 publications that have historically had the greatest citation impact according to the measure devised by Shapiro were analyzed. In particular, analysis of legal scholarship during the realignment that gave rise to the 4th Party System's Republican regime was limited to the top two law reviews in terms of historical citation impact (Harvard Law Review and Yale Law Journal), analysis of legal scholarship during the realignment that gave rise to the New Deal regime was limited to the top three law reviews in terms of historical citation impact (Columbia Law Review, Harvard Law Review, and Yale Law Journal), and analysis of legal scholarship during the realignment that gave rise to the New Right regime was limited to the top 15 law reviews in terms of historical citation impact (California Law Review, Columbia Law Review, Cornell Law Review, Duke Law Journal, Georgetown Law Journal, Harvard Law Review, Michigan Law Review, New York University Law Review, Stanford Law Review, Texas Law Review, U.C.L.A. Law Review, University of Chicago Law Review, University of Pennsylvania Law Review, Virginia Law Review, and Yale Law Journal). For each case study, a ten-year period bracketing the critical event representing the embrace of a legal ideology by prominent political actors affiliated with a new regime was examined. The law reviews were searched chronologically using the JSTOR and LexisNexis electronic archives. Every article, book review, comment, and note was read in its entirety in order to code whether it explicitly embraces or critiques the legal ideologies of interest.

Given the dynamics of the law review editorial process, it was anticipated that the effects of each of these critical events on the legal marketplace of ideas would begin to materialize within one to two years of their occurrence. It was anticipated that this would take the form of a significant increase in the amount of scholarship embracing the legal ideology associated with the new regime. It is also likely that the increased prominence of a legal ideology that challenges inherited understandings of the law would be reflected in a significant increase in the volume of scholarship attacking that ideology in the short term, as legal scholars affiliated with the old regime felt compelled to engage and challenge viewpoints that they would have previously dismissed out of hand or ignored.

With regard to the selection of the ten-year interval examined in each case study, the history of each of the three periods under consideration presents a key moment at which an existing legal intellectual movement was appropriated by a new political-electoral regime. For example, originalism had existed for a number of years as a relatively small but prominent legal countermovement to the legal liberalism of the Warren Court years prior to being elevated to the quasi-official legal ideology of the emerging New Right regime. Building upon Wechsler's critique of the Warren Court and call for a jurisprudence guided by "neutral principles," early originalist scholarship, such as the seminal work of Bork and Berger, was viewed as a decidedly radical challenge to legal orthodoxy prior to the explicit endorsement of originalism as a method of constitutional interpretation by prominent members of the Reagan administration.[51] The campaign to persuade the public that the nation's courts had erred by departing from the original intention of the Constitution's framers that was launched by Attorney General Edwin Meese's 1985 speech to the American Bar Association thus represents the critical moment at which originalism would be expected to have begun its transition from radical to mainstream and would be expected to have assumed a more prominent place in legal scholarship, the legal academy, and in constitutional discourse generally. That this campaign represented the moment of originalism's appropriation by the New Right regime is underscored by the simultaneous upsurge in anti-judicial rhetoric by the Republican Party. For example, the party's 1984 platform contained unprecedentedly strong language denouncing "an elitist and unresponsive judiciary" and promising the appointment of federal judges with a "commitment to judicial restraint."

The relationship between the rise of the New Deal regime and the rise of the legal realist movement is somewhat less straightforward. This is because legal realism, as an offshoot of the sociological legal scholarship of the Progressive Era, was better established in the legal academy prior to the construction of the New Deal regime than was originalism prior to the construction of the New Right regime.

Nonetheless, legal realism differed from sociological jurisprudence in important ways that marked it as a far more radical challenge to legal formalism, differences that prompted the legal realist movement to be viewed as an insurgency of scholars "peculiarly vocal in advocating…rebellious points of view."[52] As this movement has been widely described as the "jurisprudential analog" to the New Deal, the launch of the New Deal in 1933 represents the critical moment at which legal realism would be expected to have begun its most significant period of growth in the legal marketplace of ideas.[53] This appropriation of legal realism was signaled by the Roosevelt administration in a variety of ways that made clear that its views were in accord with those of legal realists and that it would not be bound by the rigid constitutional strictures of legal formalism. These included its frequent invocations of the concept of a living Constitution, its appointment of prominent legal realists to important posts in the administration, and its expansive reading of federal power, particularly presidential power under the emergency powers doctrine.[54]

The rise of legal formalism presents a similar puzzle. Legal formalism has been described by some scholars as the natural culmination of trends toward greater systemization and integration of legal doctrine that unfolded over the course of several decades.[55] However, there is reason to believe that the particular form that it took was a product of political developments in the 1890s that garnered broader acceptance for previously controversial doctrines such as substantive due process. The prominence of these formalist doctrines, which had first been promulgated decades earlier but which had theretofore generally been rejected by the courts and considered somewhat outside of the mainstream of legal thought, can only be understood in the context of the class conflict that defined this period in American history. It was this class conflict, which took the form of widespread labor strife and the emergence of agrarian protest movements, that led elite lawyers to express concern that the power of the state would be used by political majorities to redistribute the nation's wealth, concern that the doctrines of legal formalism were tailored to address. Moreover, legal formalism and the class conflict that helped spawn it were increasingly politicized over the course of the 1890s, culminating in the critical election of 1896. This election saw legal formalism take center stage as the Democratic Party championed economic populism and attacked formalism on the courts while the

Republican Party championed economic conservatism and embraced formalist trends in jurisprudence. Thus, it would be anticipated that the election of 1896, which resulted in a decisive victory for the Republican proponents of legal formalism that set the stage for three decades of Republican domination of national politics, would be the critical moment at which legal formalism would be expected to have begun its most significant period of growth in the legal marketplace of ideas.

Although defining legal formalism, legal realism, and originalism with precision is complicated by the multiple and sometimes contradictory strains of thought within any legal intellectual movement, a distinctive core set of principles unites each of the three so as to allow for the consistent classification of legal scholarship. For legal formalism, these principles flow from the fact that it represented an effort on the part of its proponents to transform the judicial process into a more scientific process that insulated law from politics. Reflecting a distrust of majoritarian democracy in an era of politicized class conflict that stemmed from immigration, industrialization, and urbanization, legal formalism sought to achieve this by drawing a sharp distinction between the public law of criminal and regulatory law and the private law of contract, property, and tort law, with the state's ability to reorder relations among citizens that are governed by private law circumscribed and limited to ensuring that the law is impartially administered. While formalists were therefore particularly skeptical of state action that invaded the realm of private law by regulating ostensibly private relationships such as employer-employee relationships, this skepticism also flowed from a more general fear of class legislation that used the power of the state to promote the interests of particular groups or classes rather than to promote the general welfare.[56] Formalists' desire to secure a realm of private rights insulated from an increasingly illiberal political environment also necessitated a change in the structure of legal concepts toward increasingly abstract and general principles and classifications that could provide rules of decision for the broadest possible range of cases and thereby render the law more predictable and less political.[57] The defining features of legal formalist scholarship distinguishing it from the more functionalist and pragmatic legal scholarship that preceded it are thus formalism's concept of a sharp and consequential distinction between public law and private law, its embrace of doctrines such as substantive due process that serve to prevent transgressions of this distinction by the state, and its efforts to formulate increasingly abstract and systematic general theories of areas of the law previously conceptualized as collections of disparate precedents and rules.[58]

Growing sentiment that this abstract conceptualism was insufficiently cognizant of its practical consequences ultimately gave rise to a countermovement in the form of legal realism, which, in contrast to legal formalism's efforts to separate the two, embraced the inherent connection between law and politics. The intellectual heirs to calls for a sociological jurisprudence by Progressive Era legal scholars, legal realists' attacks on legal formalism illuminated the artificial and socially constructed nature of formalist distinctions between the public and private spheres and of other traditional legal classifications and categories.[59] This anti-conceptualism was reflective of a more general skepticism of the sufficiency and desirability of relying upon abstract doctrine to decide concrete cases and a resulting emphasis upon contextualism and pragmatism in jurisprudence. This conception of the law as fundamentally ambiguous and incomplete and consequent aversion to bright line classifications and rules was most notably manifested in an aversion to individual rights claims premised upon such bright line classifications and rules.[60] It was also manifested in calls for greater judicial deference to the judgments of legislative and administrative policymakers. The defining features of legal realist scholarship are thus its efforts to deconstruct legal concepts and categorizations and to question the utility of deductive legal reasoning, its integration of considerations of social and economic utility and calls for balancing tests sensitive to the context of individual cases, and its support for state power in cases involving individual rights claims, particularly economic rights claims grounded in the doctrine of substantive due process.

Legal realism would eventually sow of the seeds of its own countermovement as it was concern that the non-interpretivist jurisprudence spawned by the rise of legal realism represented, in the words of Attorney General Meese, "policy choices [rather] than articulations of constitutional principle," that fueled calls for a return to a formalist jurisprudence in the form of originalism.[61] While modern originalism differs from earlier incarnations of legal formalism in a number of important respects, most significantly its skepticism of the recognition of unenumerated rights such as the right to privacy via the doctrine of substantive due process, originalists share with earlier legal formalists a commitment to ostensibly de-politicizing the law by restraining judicial discretion by prescribing reliance upon neutral principles as fixed points of reference.[62] Whereas conceptualism served this purpose for the first generation of legal formalists, the understanding of constitutional provisions espoused by their respective framers and shared by the people at the time of their ratification serves as the fixed point of reference of choice for originalists. While modern constitutional scholarship has rarely completely disregarded the original intention and original meaning and has generally granted them some role in narrowing the scope of possible interpretations, originalist scholarship may be distinguished by the privileged place that it accords them, viewing them, in the words of Meese and other originalists, as "the only reliable guide" capable of producing a consistent and democratically legitimate jurisprudence.[63]

The timing and magnitude of the penetration of insurgent legal ideologies into the legal marketplace of ideas was also examined from the perspective of the judicial supply-side problem identified by Teles. As Teles notes, the dominance of liberal understandings of the law in the legal profession initially made it difficult for Republican presidents to use judicial appointments to advance the New Right regime's legal agenda. However, this supply-side problem has not been limited to the New Right regime. Instead, there have numerous examples of presidents over the course of American history, particularly presidents serving early in the life cycle of political-electoral regimes, expressing disappointment with the jurisprudence of their judicial nominees. In order to assess the dynamics of the supply-side problem during each of these three regimes and its relationship to the entrenchment of those regimes' legal ideologies in the legal profession, an analysis of Supreme Court appointments was conducted. In particular, using Schmidhauser's ideological typology classifying justices that served during the 4th Party System and Martin and Quinn's estimations of the ideal points in ideological space for justices that served during the New Deal regime and have served during the New Right regime, this analysis examined the extent to which generational replacement has driven ideological change on the Court.[64]

It was anticipated that each regime would face a supply-side problem early in its life cycle as it was forced to draw judicial nominees from a legal profession whose members' understandings of the law had been shaped under the previous regime. However, it was anticipated that this problem would wane as the passage of time resulted in judicial nominees increasingly being drawn from the ranks of lawyers whose legal education and professionalization had occurred after the displacement of the previous regime, when the takeover of the legal marketplace of ideas and profession by the new regime's legal ideology was underway. Thus, Republican presidents should have had more consistent success in appointing conservative jurists later in the life cycle of the New Right regime as the older generations of lawyers whose legal education and professionalization had occurred during the heyday of legal realism and of the Warren Court were replaced by a new generation of lawyers whose legal education and professionalization had occurred during the period of conservative backlash against political and legal liberalism. Similarly, Democratic presidents should have had more consistent success in appointing liberal jurists later in the life cycle of the New Deal regime as the older generation of lawyers whose legal education and professionalization had occurred during the ascendancy of legal formalism was replaced by a new generation of lawyers that had been inculcated with a more realist understanding of the law. Republican presidents should also have had more consistent success in appointing conservative jurists later in the life cycle of the 4th Party System as the older generation of lawyers whose legal education and professionalization had occurred during the heyday of 19th century legal thought's more functional and pragmatic approach to the law was replaced by a new generation of lawyers that had been imbued with the tenets of legal formalism.

The process by which regimes' legal ideologies take over the legal profession was also measured via a variety of more qualitative methods that triangulated the findings of the analysis of trends in elite law reviews and the analysis of Supreme Court appointments. These included surveys of developments in legal education during each of the three periods being examined. Of particular interest were curricula, pedagogy, and faculty hiring at elite law schools, each of which underwent significant change congruent with changes in the legal marketplace of ideas during each of the three periods. They also included analysis of legal academic responses to the major works of prominent scholars associated with the legal intellectual movements under examination, such as realists Jerome Frank and Karl Llewellyn and originalists Raoul Berger and Robert Bork. Of particular interest was the manner in which the tone of these responses evolved over time as the legal ideologies that these scholars represented found broader acceptance in the legal profession.

By measuring the timing and magnitude of rising legal intellectual movements' penetrations of the legal marketplace of ideas and placing them in the context of trends in electoral politics, constitutional dialogue, and legal education, this book makes an important contribution to the understanding of the complex relationship between political and legal change. By linking these changes in the legal marketplace of ideas to changes in the dynamics of judicial appointments, it also provides insight into how political-electoral regimes are able to entrench their constitutional visions in the courts. This book also offers new insight into the dynamics of issue evolution by illustrating the manner in which cues from political elites not only structure mass political behavior but also structure intellectual debates. Perhaps most importantly, it suggests limitations to progressive theories of law that view litigation as an instrument for the achievement of social reform by illustrating how politics shapes the prism through which the law is interpreted.[65] However, while this may be discouraging to those who seek to use the courts to achieve social change, it ultimately underscores the democratic legitimacy of judicial review and provides further illustration that it should not be conceptualized as a counter-majoritarian force. As judicial outputs are reflective of the balance of opinion in the legal marketplace of ideas, the fact that that marketplace of ideas has not been insular but rather has been responsive to changes in electoral politics should be viewed approvingly.

CHAPTER 2

Originalism and the New Right Regime

INTRODUCTION

"Are we all originalists now?" asks the introduction to a 2007 symposium on constitutional law.[1] While the question may seem absurd on its face given the acrimonious debate that has raged in the legal academy, the courts, and the political arena between proponents of originalism and proponents of a living Constitution, it illustrates the success that proponents of originalism have had in changing the terms of constitutional debate in the United States. The fact that even some of the legal scholars most strongly identified with the concept of a living Constitution, such as Ronald Dworkin and Jack Balkin, have recently been "dressing up their theories in the garb of originalism" indicates that a significant paradigm shift has occurred.[2] This paradigm shift is particularly remarkable given the place of originalism in the legal marketplace of ideas only a few decades ago, when there were "precious few originalists of any stripe in the academy."[3] While the newfound prominence of originalism fits into a historical pattern of political change, in this case the rise of the New Right political-electoral regime, being accompanied by legal change, the causal order of events linking conservative trends in national politics to these changes in the legal marketplace of ideas has been the subject of debate. In order to better understand the connection between the rise of the New Right regime and the increasingly prominent place of originalism in constitutional discourse, this chapter analyzes the temporal relationship between conservative legal mobilization, the efforts of the Reagan administration to promote originalism, the growth in the amount of originalist scholarship published in elite law reviews, and other indicators of originalism's increased standing in the legal profession. It finds that conservative legal mobilization was by itself insufficient to significantly impact constitutional discourse and that originalism did not gain widespread acceptance until after originalism was embraced by the New Right regime.

THE RISE OF THE NEW RIGHT REGIME

The term "New Right regime" refers to the period of Republican ascendancy in national politics that began with the election of 1968, an election that saw enduring changes in the political climate and in voting patterns that many political scientists have argued mark the end of the New Deal regime.[4] The most significant of these changes was the emergence of a Republican advantage in presidential elections, with Republican candidates winning seven of the last 12 presidential elections (1968, 1972, 1980, 1984, 1988, 2000, and 2004). This represents a reversal of the dynamics of presidential elections during the New Deal regime, when the Democratic Party enjoyed a virtual lock on the presidency and Republican candidates won only two of the nine presidential elections between 1932 and 1964 (1952 and 1956), and a reprise of the dynamics of presidential elections during the 4th Party System, when Republican candidates won seven of the nine presidential elections held between 1896 and 1928 (1896, 1900, 1904, 1908, 1920, 1924, and 1928). However, the new political-electoral regime that the election of 1968 ushered in differed from previous regimes insofar as the Republican Party's dominance in presidential elections did not immediately translate to dominance in congressional elections. While the Democratic Party simultaneously controlled both houses of Congress for 32 of the 36 years of the New Deal regime and the Republican Party simultaneously controlled both houses of Congress for 26 of the 36 years of the 4th Party System, there have only been ten years of complete Republican control of Congress since 1968 and the first of these did not come until after the 1994 elections. Indeed, over the course of the New Right regime the Republican Party has held an average of only 194 seats in the House of Representatives and only 47 seats in the Senate while the Democratic Party has held an average of 240 seats in the House of Representatives and 53 seats in the Senate.

The New Right regime is also weaker than previous regimes in terms of macro-partisanship. Although the percentage of Americans identifying as Democrats has declined significantly since the 1960s,

Table 2.1: Partisan Control of Political Institutions during the New Right Regime

Congress (Years)	*House of Representatives (Party Breakdown)*	*Senate (Party Breakdown)*	*Presidency (President)*	*Control*
91st (1969-71)	Democratic (243-192)	Democratic (57-43)	Republican (Nixon)	Divided
92nd (1971-73)	Democratic (255-180)	Democratic (54-44-1-1)	Republican (Nixon)	Divided
93rd (1973-75)	Democratic (242-192-1)	Democratic (56-42-1-1)	Republican (Nixon/Ford)	Divided
94th (1975-77)	Democratic (291-144)	Democratic (61-37-1-1)	Republican (Ford)	Divided
95th (1977-79)	Democratic (292-143)	Democratic (61-38-1)	Democratic (Carter)	Opposition
96th (1979-81)	Democratic (277-158)	Democratic (58-41-1)	Democratic (Carter)	Opposition
97th (1981-83)	Democratic (242-192-1)	Republican (53-46-1)	Republican (Reagan)	Divided
98th (1983-85)	Democratic (269-166)	Republican (55-45)	Republican (Reagan)	Divided
99th (1985-87)	Democratic (253-182)	Republican (53-47)	Republican (Reagan)	Divided
100th (1987-89)	Democratic (258-177)	Democratic (55-45)	Republican (Reagan)	Divided
101st (1989-91)	Democratic (260-175)	Democratic (55-45)	Republican (G.H.W. Bush)	Divided
102nd (1991-93)	Democratic (267-167-1)	Democratic (56-44)	Republican (G.H.W. Bush)	Divided
103rd (1993-95)	Democratic (258-176-1)	Democratic (57-43)	Democratic (Clinton)	Opposition
104th (1995-97)	Republican (230-204-1)	Republican (53-47)	Democratic (Clinton)	Divided
105th (1997-99)	Republican (228-206-1)	Republican (55-45)	Democratic (Clinton)	Divided
106th (1999-2001)	Republican (223-211-1)	Republican (55-45)	Democratic (Clinton)	Divided
107th (2001-03)	Republican (221-212-2)	Democratic (50-49-1)	Republican (G.W. Bush)	Divided
108th (2003-05)	Republican (229-205-1)	Republican (51-48-1)	Republican (G.W. Bush)	Complete
109th (2005-07)	Republican (232-202-1)	Republican (55-44-1)	Republican (G.W. Bush)	Complete
110th (2007-09)	Democratic (233-202)	Democratic (49-49-1-1)	Republican (G.W. Bush)	Divided
111th (2009-11)	Democratic (257-178)	Democratic (57-41-1-1)	Democratic (Obama)	Opposition
112th (2011-13)	Republican (242-193)	Democratic (51-47-1-1)	Democratic (Obama)	Divided
113th (2013-15)	Republican (234-201)	Democratic (53-45-2)	Democratic (Obama)	Divided
114th (2015-17)	Republican (247-188)	Republican (54-44-2)	Democratic (Obama)	Divided

there has been no corresponding increase in the number of Americans identifying as Republicans and the number of Republican identifiers has continued to trail the number of Democratic identifiers throughout the duration of the New Right regime.[5] Instead, the most significant trend in macro-partisanship during the New Right regime has been the increasing percentage of Americans who identify as independents. This has led many political scientists to conclude that new dynamics are at work that have changed the nature of partisanship and that make the New Right regime qualitatively different from previous regimes.[6] Illustrative of these new dynamics is the unprecedented incidence of divided government during the New Right regime. While there were only eight years of divided government during the New Deal regime and only six years of divided government during the 4th Party System, there have been 32 years of divided government during the New Right regime, making divided government the most common arrangement by far during this period.

This lack of a decisive reconstruction of the political order was reflected in the regime's somewhat tentative rise in the late 1960s. As a destabilizing confluence of "ghetto riots, campus riots, street crime, anti-Vietnam marches, poor people's marches, drugs, pornography, welfarism, [and] rising taxes" led to a backlash against the liberalism of the Democratic Party, the Republican Party capitalized by seizing upon the issue of "law and order."[7] However, unlike the large victories won by new majority parties in previous realigning elections, Richard Nixon won the presidency in 1968 with only 43% of the popular vote in a three-way race while the Democratic Party retained large majorities in both houses of Congress. Nonetheless, as nearly 60% of the popular vote had been cast for the two conservative candidates in the race, many saw the election results as heralding the arrival of a new regime. These most notably included Nixon advisor Kevin Phillips, whose analysis in *The Emerging Republican Majority* would serve as a blueprint for subsequent Republican efforts to permanently realign the electorate.[8] Central to these efforts was Nixon's "Southern strategy," which attempted to appeal to the Southern Democrats who had supported third party candidate George Wallace in 1968 through rhetorical support for states' rights and opposition to busing. More generally, Republicans attempted to appeal to a broad segment of traditionalists alienated by the Democratic Party by emphasizing a complex of new moral, social, and religious issues.

Yet despite Nixon's vision of a new conservative majority that would unite economic and social conservatives, his actual record as president was characterized by accommodation of the liberal consensus of the New Deal regime. This was true not only in domestic policy, where Nixon imposed wage and price controls, instituted affirmative action in federal hiring and contracting, and established the Environmental Protection Agency, but also in foreign policy, where Nixon ended the Vietnam War and pursued a policy of détente with the communist bloc. Moreover, although Nixon enjoyed a landslide reelection victory in 1972 over another weak Democratic opponent perceived as the representative of a "liberal 'elite' that was out of step with the rest of the country," this was a personal victory that did not redound to the benefit of Republican congressional candidates or the Republican Party.[9] However, Nixon's subsequent resignation as a result of the Watergate scandal was not merely a personal defeat and represented a significant setback for the nascent New Right regime, precipitating large Democratic gains in both houses of Congress and a significant decline in the percentage of Republican identifiers in the electorate and setting the stage for Jimmy Carter's victory in the 1976 presidential election.

It was not until 1980 that the stalled realignment would regain momentum as the Republican Party would mount a more comprehensive and successful challenge to the ideology of the New Deal regime under the leadership of Ronald Reagan. Reagan's calls to cut taxes, reduce the size and regulatory power of the federal government, and pursue a more aggressively anti-communist foreign policy and his embrace of conservative positions on a host of social issues would fundamentally change the terms of debate in American politics.[10] In particular, this articulation of a clearer contrast between the two parties sharply accelerated the realignment of the electorate. Whereas previous Republican presidents such as Dwight Eisenhower, Richard Nixon, and Gerald Ford had attempted to accommodate the liberal consensus of the New Deal regime by blurring ideological distinctions, under Reagan conservatism increasingly assumed the political offensive. Consequently, while Americans' positions on fiscal, economic, and role of government issues had constituted the major partisan cleavage during the New Deal regime, a cleavage that was strongly class-based, a new social-cultural partisan cleavage between liberals and traditionalists began to emerge. Moreover, over the life cycle of the New Right regime this cleavage has increasingly displaced the older cleavage as the religious right and other groups committed to a more populist brand of conservatism have become increasingly powerful within the Republican Party.[11] The defection of a significant bloc of socially conservative Democrats that this entailed cemented the Republican advantage in presidential elections as Republicans won landslide victories in the elections of 1980, 1984, and 1988 and more modest victories in the elections of 2000 and 2004.

Despite this advantage in recent presidential elections, the New Right regime has, like previous regimes, been vulnerable to national crises and divisions within its own ranks that have allowed opposition candidates to capture the presidency. Not only was Bill Clinton able to win the presidency in 1992 amidst the economic recession of the early 1990s and conservative disaffection with George H.W. Bush that spawned the third party candidacy of H. Ross Perot, Barack Obama was able to capture the presidency in 2008 amidst the economic recession and financial crisis of the late 2000s and growing public weariness of the Iraq War. While Obama's place in political time remains the subject of debate, there is general agreement that Clinton, who memorably declared that the era of "big government" was over, was a preemptive president who was forced to adapt to the zeitgeist of the New Right regime.[12] Moreover, in each case the New Right regime has demonstrated its resiliency by capturing congressional majorities that have constrained these presidents' abilities to construct a more liberal political order.

The fact that Republicans were able to win majorities in both houses of Congress for the first time in over 40 years in 1994 and subsequently regain their majority in the House of Representatives in 2010 and in the Senate in 2014 illustrates how the New Right regime was eventually able to translate its dominance in presidential elections into congressional majorities. That the New Right regime was in its third decade before it was able to control Congress reflects in large part the unique and gradual nature of the realignment of the South. Although Republicans were carrying most of region's states in presidential elections from the very birth of the New Right regime, the depth of the region's historical attachment to the Democratic Party and the ability of local Democratic politicians to distance themselves from the liberalism of their national party meant that the region continued to send mostly moderate and conservative Democrats to Congress until relatively recently.[13] Indeed, a majority of the region's seats in both the House of Representatives and the Senate were held by Democrats as late as 1994. These Southern Democrats constituted an ideologically distinctive bloc in Congress that formed shifting coalitions with Northern Democrats and Republicans for much of the New Deal and New Right regimes.[14] Their gradual replacement by Republicans (and the concurrent replacement of liberal Northern Republicans by Democrats) has given the New Right regime a more ideologically coherent and polarized party system in which conservative majorities have organized Congress under the Republican label.

THE INSUFFICIENCY OF CONSERVATIVE LEGAL MOBILIZATION

Just as the New Right regime represents the most recent in a historical pattern of oscillation between conservative and liberal trends in national politics, the rise of originalism in constitutional discourse represents the most recent episode in a historical pattern of oscillation between formalist and instrumentalist trends in legal thought. As O'Neill explains, the originalism that was first brought to bear upon contemporary constitutional controversies by legal scholars such as Robert Bork and Raoul Berger is best understood as a modern incarnation of the "textual originalism" that pervaded constitutional law prior to its displacement by legal realism.[15] Moreover, just as this earlier incarnation of originalism was ultimately marginalized by its association with an increasingly unpopular jurisprudence at odds with the political climate of its time, the instrumentalist jurisprudence that replaced it on the courts and in the academy would sow its own countermovement when it came into conflict with a new political-electoral regime. It was this conflict between the Warren Court's "liberal" jurisprudence and the political and constitutional commitments of the emerging conservative electoral majority that emerged after the realigning election of 1968 that set the stage for the reemergence of originalism as a significant mode of constitutional thought and argument. The originalist guise that the conservative legal countermovement took was a reflection of the fact that the Warren Court invited critique rooted in historical analysis by repudiating numerous well-established constitutional doctrines and replacing them with constitutional interpretations rooted in sociological analysis that appeared to be at odds with original constitutional meanings.

However, as Teles illustrates, the ability of this originalist countermovement to penetrate the legal marketplace of ideas was limited by the presence of a "liberal legal network" that dominated the legal academy and public interest law and served as an enduring relic of the New Deal regime that was seemingly impervious to political change.[16] This dominance was the product of a unique confluence of events in the years following World War II. Perhaps the most important of these events was the wave of expansion that swept the nation's law schools. This was significant insofar as it led to an influx of new faculty whose previous experience had been as government lawyers during the New Deal, faculty who brought distinctive perspectives on the law to the classroom. This represented the first step in the progressive liberalization of law school faculty. It was also a first step in the liberalization of law schools' student bodies insofar as it opened these schools' doors to an increasingly diverse range of students in terms of gender, race, and socioeconomic status.

The seeds of the liberal legal network were also planted during this period by the increasing success of public interest law firms in using sustained litigation campaigns to achieve legal change. As Teles notes, the early successes of the N.A.A.C.P. Legal Defense and Educational Fund and the American Civil Liberties Union were critical to fostering a "vision of the role of the lawyer in progressive struggles," one that had a "profound cultural impact on the profession."[17] This vision was legitimated by the jurisprudence of the Warren Court, whose decisive break with the tradition of judicial restraint that had guided the Court since the New Deal did much to change attitudes in the legal profession toward the use of litigation as a means of bringing about social change. Indeed, as Kalman illustrates, as a result of the Court's central role in spearheading such social change "the law seemed like a romance."[18] This changing understanding of the law revolutionized the way that legal education was marketed, with law schools attempting to capitalize upon the excitement that the Warren Court generated among liberals by producing "glossy admissions brochures entic[ing]...students into law school with promises that lawyers of the future, riding white chargers, will crusade against social problems."[19]

These developments would significantly change the ideological composition of law school student bodies as the image of the legal profession was transformed and it increasingly became a profession that appealed to liberals. This transformation was particularly pronounced at elite law schools, whose students disproportionately gravitated toward the careers in public interest law that were becoming an ever more popular alternative to traditional corporate practice. This ideological shift among law students corresponded to a second surge in hiring in the nation's law schools that saw the number of full-time law professors more than double between 1962 and 1977.[20] As a result, law schools experienced an additional influx of new faculty whose political views were on average well to the left of their senior colleagues. This influx would further change the character of the legal academy and of legal education. Whereas law professors had historically been more conservative than their counterparts in the humanities and social sciences, by the 1990s their political attitudes had become indistinguishable.[21] This new generation of law professors used their position to advance a vision of the law that reflected the spirit of the Warren Court, one in which decisions such as *Brown v. Board of Education* and *Roe v. Wade* represented the "text of a new civil religion."[22] This vision differed significantly from that of the older generation of law professors insofar as it wholeheartedly embraced judicial activism and did not struggle with the counter-majoritarian difficulty of judicial review, a struggle that had consumed law professors who came of age during the New Deal. Buoyed by generational replacement and by the changing role conception of the legal profession, this liberal constitutional vision soon achieved a "dominance so complete that every casebook, treatise, and handbook used to teach constitutional law in American law schools [was] the product of Democrats writing from Democratic perspectives."[23]

The legacy of the Warren Court was also reflected in changing law school curricula, which increasingly included clinical components that allowed students to engage in the sort of politically conscious lawyering that the Warren Court had glamorized. This newfound emphasis upon clinical training came in response to widespread calls from leading members of the profession for legal education to have greater practical relevance and in response to the Supreme Court's decision in *Gideon v. Wainwright*, which recognized a constitutional right to state-appointed counsel for indigent criminal defendants and led the American Bar Association to call upon law schools to expand legal aid programs. The resulting expansion of these programs would represent another critical facet of the liberalization of American legal education. This was because the type of legal work that students performed in these clinical programs frequently had a distinct ideological tenor and provided the growing ranks of liberal public interest law firms with a critical supply of free labor. Indeed, these programs were highly politicized from the outset, with their oft-stated commitment to "social justice" reflected in their participation in politically controversial litigation. Thus, they have consistently drawn the ire of conservatives, such as MacDonald, who credits law school clinics with, among other dubious accomplishments, "setting up needle exchanges for drug addicts in residential neighborhoods…allowing female murderers to beat the rap by claiming 'battered women's syndrome'…and preventing…libraries from ejecting foul-smelling vagrants who are disturbing library users."[24] The politicization of clinical education has been such that at many law schools, particularly elite law schools, a "majority of clinics have a recognizable leftist or identity politics mission."[25]

The growth of these programs was fueled not only by demand from students and the legal profession but also by significant financial support from private foundations, particularly the Ford Foundation. After supporting efforts to expand access to legal services for the poor for more than a decade, the Ford Foundation's 1969 initiative to fund clinical education in law schools played a major role in the nationwide expansion of these programs. The Ford Foundation also provided seed money for a diverse array of public interest law firms. These included civil rights law firms such as the N.A.A.C.P. Legal Defense and Educational Fund and the Mexican American Legal Defense and Educational Fund, civil liberties law firms such as the American Civil Liberties Union's Women's Rights Project, and environmental law firms such as the Natural Resources Defense Council and the Sierra Club Legal Defense Fund.[26] This early work in funding liberal public interest law quickly became a model for other private foundations, which provided a critical support structure for the liberal legal mobilization that was unfolding. For example, shortly thereafter the Carnegie endowment directed its philanthropic efforts toward funding the litigation that forced the introduction of bilingual education in public schools while the Edna McConnell Clark Foundation, established by the heirs to the Avon fortune, played a key role in funding the litigation that forced the mass de-institutionalization of mental patients.[27]

This financial support was made possible by change in the strategic vision of private foundations that saw such foundations de-emphasize direct assistance to the needy and instead emphasize the "financing of adversarial politics and insurgent organizing."[28] However, such was the depth of the "prevailing liberal consensus in elite circles and institutions" that these efforts generally were not perceived by their sponsors in ideological terms.[29] Instead, the movement to liberalize the legal profession and use law to advance a liberal policy agenda was, at least initially, "strangely uncontroversial."[30] Indeed, it had the support and cooperation of the traditionally conservative "white-shoe lawyers" of the corporate bar, many of whom served on the boards of these private foundations and de-politicized the public image of their litigation efforts.[31] Thus, the Ford Foundation's McGeorge Bundy could confidently declare that "there was only one right side to the question of equal opportunity" when the propriety of philanthropic institutions sponsoring such politically charged litigation was questioned.[32]

The result of this liberal hold over the institutions that shape legal orthodoxy and set the courts' agenda was an inability of the New Right regime to translate its political values and commitments into legal change. Teles argues that this began to change as conservatives constructed their own support structure for legal mobilization. Perhaps the key component of this support structure in terms of the legal academy and its linkage to the courts was the Federalist Society, the conservative professional organization that was founded in 1982 with the aim of "changing legal culture through the education, recruitment, and development of young conservative lawyers."[33] The Federalist Society's efforts to change the legal profession from within and to provide an alternative for lawyers dissatisfied with the liberalism of the American Bar Association paralleled the earlier efforts of the National Lawyers Guild, which was founded in the early years of the New Deal regime to liberalize the legal profession and to provide an alternative for lawyers dissatisfied with the conservatism that then characterized the American Bar Association. The Federalist Society's initial contributions to the conservative legal movement consisted largely of changing the terms of constitutional debate by publicizing legal theories such as originalism.[34] However, over time the professional networking that the Federalist Society facilitated also created new opportunities for conservatives in the legal academy and provided Republican presidential administrations with a pool of reliably conservative lawyers to fill important positions in the executive and judicial branches.[35] The Federalist Society also played a significant role in staffing the increasing number of conservative public interest law firms that were essential to translating a federal judiciary more sympathetic to originalist arguments as a result of Republican control of the presidency into originalist constitutional jurisprudence through coordinated and sustained litigation campaigns.[36] These processes are central to the bottom-up model presented by Teles, a model driven by legal entrepreneurs creating support structures that transform the institutions such as the legal academy and the interest group system that in turn shape legal thought and jurisprudence. In a similar vein, others have illustrated the importance of publications such as National Review and think tanks such as the American Enterprise Institute and the Heritage Foundation as support structures that incubated conservative thought during the early years of the New Right regime.[37]

However, despite the importance of legal mobilization, there is reason to believe that the dynamics of legal change are characterized by a more top-down process. Perhaps the most apposite criticism that has been leveled against Teles is his overstatement of the success and influence of the conservative legal movement.[38] As Teles concedes and as has been illustrated in greater detail by other studies, the faculties of the elite law schools that play a disproportionate role in shaping legal thought are as overwhelmingly liberal today as they were prior to the supposed "rise" of the conservative legal movement.[39] Similarly, conservative public interest law firms, not only in terms of their overall number but also in terms of their funding, the number of lawyers that they employ, and the amount of litigation that they sponsor, continue to be dwarfed by liberal public interest law firms despite the efforts of "success stories" such as the Center for Individual Rights and the Institute for Justice.[40] This suggests that the origins of originalism's newfound prominence in constitutional discourse are to be found not at the micro level of legal entrepreneurs but at the macro level of national politics.

THE ROLE OF POLITICAL ELITES

As Sunstein observes, "the election returns…set the academic agenda" and the emergence of new trends in legal thought can generally be attributed to "external shocks" from the world of politics.[41] This stems from what Barnhizer has characterized as the "faddishness" of legal scholarship and its willingness to take its cues from figures in positions of institutional authority.[42] In particular, as Barnhizer notes, "legal scholars…spend…much time trying to figure out the current 'hot topic' so that their writing can fit into an acceptable pattern."[43] As a result, "the more powerful and influential the people who are willing to make a legal argument, the more quickly it moves from the positively loony to the positively thinkable."[44] Thus, in understanding the transformation of the place of originalism in the legal marketplace of ideas from marginal countermovement to mainstream constitutional theory it is necessary to consider the broader political context. In particular, it is necessary to consider the effect of the external shock caused by the explicit embrace of originalism by the Reagan administration. Not only did the Reagan administration make a strong rhetorical commitment to originalism through Attorney General Edwin Meese's campaign for a "jurisprudence of original intention," it also subsequently followed through on this rhetorical commitment by nominating prominent originalist scholar Robert Bork to the Supreme Court. This represented a dramatic escalation of previous Republican presidential administrations' vague criticisms of the courts and precipitated an intense constitutional debate whose effects on the legal marketplace of ideas have been insufficiently analyzed.

The first precursors to these efforts to promote originalism date to the rise of the New Right regime and Richard Nixon's 1968 presidential campaign. One of the major themes of Nixon's campaign was opposition to the Warren Court's landmark criminal procedure decisions, articulated by Nixon as a defense of law and order. Moreover, Nixon also frequently spoke more generally of the need to reorient the Supreme Court's approach to constitutional interpretation through the appointment of "strict constructionists."[45] However, the definition of a strict constructionist jurisprudence would remain nebulous and it would never be specifically framed by Nixon or by his surrogates as an originalist jurisprudence. That Nixon's criticism of the Warren Court did not necessarily signal an embrace of originalism is reflected in the fact that none of Nixon's appointments to the Supreme Court, with the arguable exception of William Rehnquist, would exhibit any consistent interest in originalism as method of constitutional interpretation.[46] Nonetheless, Nixon's appointments to the Court were relatively united in terms of their more conservative approach to criminal procedure and school desegregation cases.[47] This reflected Nixon's broader strategy for forging a new Republican majority, which was for his administration to use crime and busing as wedge issues to divide the New Deal coalition while tempering its conservatism to avoid alienating moderate Republicans.[48] Moreover, Nixon's appointments did move the Court significantly to the right as each of these appointments was significantly more conservative than the justice that they replaced.[49] However, despite their generally more conservative records, they otherwise did little to lead a retreat from the activism of the Warren Court. Instead, they more often provided the critical votes for new exercises in activism such as *Roe v. Wade*. Consequently, Nixon's attempt to remake the Court has often been characterized as a "counter-revolution that wasn't."[50]

Consequently, dissatisfaction with the courts among leaders of the New Right regime would persist through the 1970s and early 1980s despite Republican appointees constituting a majority of the members of the Supreme Court and a growing percentage of judges sitting on lower federal courts. This inability to translate control of nominations to the federal judiciary into jurisprudential change would culminate in the most serious attempts since Reconstruction to use the powers granted Congress by Article III §2's Exceptions Clause to restrict the federal judiciary's jurisdiction. Although none ultimately passed, the fact that bills such as Senator John East's Judicial Reform Bill, which would have effectively repealed the doctrine of incorporation by prohibiting the Supreme Court from hearing cases involving alleged violations of the Bill of Rights by state and local governments, were introduced and received serious consideration during this period indicates the climate that existed at the time.[51]

The New Right regime's dissatisfaction with the courts is also illustrated by the change in the tone of the rhetoric of the Republican Party during the Reagan era (see Figure 2.1). This change was measured by coding references to the courts in Republican Party platforms from 1968 to 1988 as negative, neutral, or positive. Negative references comprised all references to the courts that directly critique their membership and/or jurisprudence, such as the 1980 platform's assertion that President Carter's "appointments to federal judgeships have been particularly disappointing" and the 1988 platform's assertion that federal courts have "undermine[d] the stature of the judiciary and erode[d] respect for the rule of law." In contrast, neutral references comprised references to the courts that represent general statements of principle regarding legal policy and/or judicial appointments, such as the 1972 platform's pledge to appoint to the Supreme Court "lawyers of firm judicial temperament and fidelity to the Constitution," while positive references comprised references to the courts that specifically praised their membership and/or jurisprudence, such as the 1988 platform's statement "commending the Reagan-Bush team for naming to the federal courts distinguished women and men committed to judicial restraint, the rights of law-abiding citizens, and traditional family values." The numbers of negative and neutral/positive references to the courts are expressed as the percentages comprised by those references of the total number of words in each Republican Party platform.

Figure 2.1: References to the Courts in Republican Party Platforms,

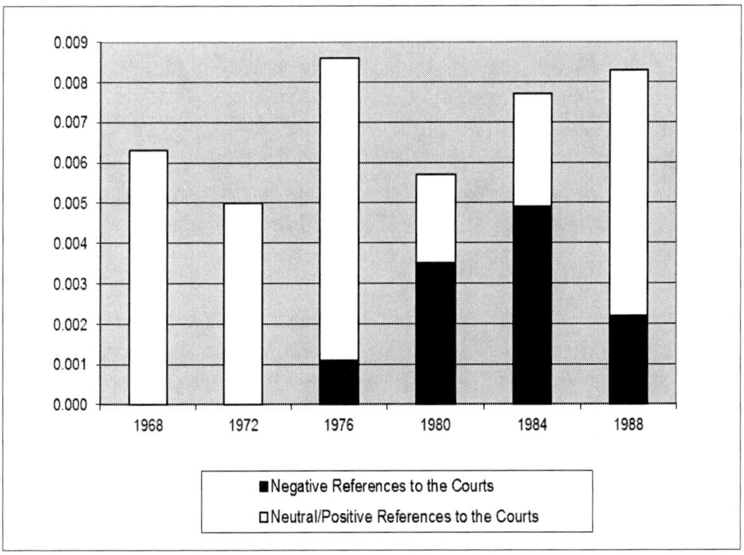

The relative frequency of such references over time illustrates a clear trend. In particular, references to the courts in Republican Party platforms prior to the 1980s were relatively few in number and largely limited to boilerplate language and occasional expressions of disagreement with particular decisions. For example, despite the often harsh criticisms of the courts by Richard Nixon and his surrogates during the 1968 campaign, the language of the 1968 Republican Party platform is relatively restrained on this subject. While its references to "law and order" were widely recognized as implicit criticism of the courts, its only direct reference to the courts was its call for the "application of the highest standards in making appointments to the courts…to rebuild and enhance public respect for the Supreme Court." Indeed, the only direct criticism of the courts prior to 1980 would come in 1976 with the platform's protest of the "the Supreme Court's intrusion into the family structure through its denial of the parents' obligation and right to guide their minor children." However, as the leadership of the Republican Party became increasingly frustrated with the continued liberal bent of the courts, its focus would shift from substantive issues such as crime and family values to structural issues such as the institutional power of the judiciary and the proper role of the courts in the American political system. Thus, the 1980 and 1984 platforms are replete with strong and unprecedented criticisms of the courts that reflect the Reagan administration's desire for more fundamental legal change. This is particularly true of the 1984 platform. Denouncing "an elitist and unresponsive federal judiciary" and pledging the appointment of federal judges who "share [a] commitment to judicial restraint" and "respect the people's interest in a stable, orderly society," it takes direct aim at the Warren and Burger Courts' sweeping uses of judicial power by asserting that "it is not a judicial function to reorder the economic, political, and social priorities of our nation." Moreover, it also indicates that the party was not content to rely solely upon the appointment of federal judges committed to judicial restraint to remedy what it perceived as illegitimate judicial activism, endorsing the aforementioned "congressional efforts to restrict the jurisdiction of federal courts." These themes would be reiterated in the 1988 platform, which lays out the party's positions regarding the courts in a section pointedly entitled "Restoring the Constitution," and in subsequent platforms, which would be more explicit in their support for originalism.

The fact that the New Right regime continued to regard the federal judiciary as a hostile institution into the 1990s despite having appointed such a large proportion of its membership reflects the supply-side problem identified by Teles. As Teles notes, judges are "unusually sensitive to the dominant opinion in the legal community."[52] Given that the dominant opinion in the legal community was the legal liberalism that had served as legal orthodoxy since the Warren Court, the New Right regime was constrained in its ability to nominate judges committed to its legal agenda and even when it did those judges were constrained in their ability to credibly advance that agenda. Changing this dynamic would require not only the creation of a conservative legal network that would supply the New Right regime with a pool of reliably conservative judges and public interest lawyers but also the articulation of an alternative constitutional vision in clearer terms.

The first, and most significant, step toward creating a conservative legal network that would act as a support structure for the New Right regime was taken with the founding of the Federalist Society in 1982. Founded via the merger of a number of organizations of conservative law students at elite law schools, the Federalist Society's initial ambitions were modest and largely limited to sponsoring symposia bringing conservative perspectives on the law to institutions from which they had long been absent.[53] However, as the Federalist Society began to expand to law schools across the country and develop into an influential national network of conservative lawyers, its potential as a resource for the New Right regime was soon recognized. As a result, close but informal ties between the Federalist Society and the Reagan administration began to develop and membership "quickly became a prerequisite for law students seeking clerkships with…Reagan judicial appointees as well as for employment in the…Justice Department."[54] The Federalist Society also contributed to the New Right regime's efforts to initiate a legal counter-revolution by introducing conservative legal scholarship into the legal marketplace of ideas through the sponsorship of its own alternative publications. Thus, the Harvard Journal of Law and Public Policy, which had been founded in 1978 by a group of conservative law students who would go on to become early members of the Federalist Society, was adopted as the official publication of the Federalist Society and has been a prominent outlet for critiques of legal liberalism.[55]

Although this emerging conservative legal movement was united in its opposition to legal liberalism, its vague calls for judicial restraint and strict construction failed to present a true constitutional vision. As Stephen Markman, the founder of the Federalist Society's Washington, D.C. lawyers division, observes, this "old Nixonian terminology" was a "clumsy way of referring to…ideas."[56] This messaging problem would be overcome in large part by the efforts of the Federalist Society, which helped the conservative legal movement develop a more consistent and coherent message by facilitating contacts and exchanges among conservative legal scholars. For a number of reasons, this message would be a call for an originalist jurisprudence. Perhaps the most significant of these was the fact that originalism represented the strand that could logically tie together disparate conservative critiques of the jurisprudence of the Warren Court. As Kersch illustrates, the idea of fidelity to the original meaning of the Constitution provided a principled basis for criticizing the perceived excesses of liberal judges and underlay an emerging conservative narrative of a "virtuous demos arrayed against an ideologically driven, anti-democratic, law-wielding elite."[57] Moreover, as an originalist jurisprudence would appeal to economic conservatives by limiting the size and regulatory power of the federal government as well as appeal to social conservatives by overturning a host of Warren and Burger Court precedents in the areas of criminal procedure, privacy, and religion, originalism was touted by a number of figures on the New Right as a unifying principle that could be embraced by all of the diverse elements comprising the New Right coalition. Nonetheless, as Post and Siegel illustrate, this embrace of history as a source of constitutional meaning has often been quite selective and is perhaps best understood in the context of efforts by the New Right to "forg[e] a living connection between the Constitution and contemporary conservative ideals."[58] In this respect it represents another episode in what Rakove calls the ongoing "American search for a usable past."[59]

Yet despite its various appeals, it was not until 1985 that this unifying principle would be explicitly endorsed by the Reagan administration as the New Right's answer to legal liberalism. Perhaps the critical event that finally spurred the Reagan administration into an open embrace of the aims of the conservative legal movement was the resignation of Attorney General William French Smith following President Reagan's reelection and his replacement by Edwin Meese.

Whereas Smith had been perceived as a moderate Republican and a member of the legal establishment, Meese was strongly committed to the New Right's revolutionary legal agenda and had close ties to the Federalist Society and other arms of the conservative legal movement.[60] Thus, Meese wasted little time in using the rhetorical powers of his office to advance this agenda. Meese's declaration in his 1985 speech to the American Bar Association that "constitutional jurisprudence...should be a jurisprudence of original intention" transformed originalism from a constitutional theory espoused by a small minority of legal scholars to the centerpiece of the Reagan administration's legal agenda.[61] Moreover, this general endorsement of originalism was accompanied by a clear commitment to using the powers of the Department of Justice to advance it in the courts, with Meese pledging in the same speech that "in the cases we file and those we join as amicus, we will endeavor to resurrect the original meaning of...constitutional provisions as the only reliable guide for judgment."[62] Perhaps most importantly, Meese's remarks clearly delineated how a jurisprudence of original intention would depart significantly from Supreme Court precedent, questioning the soundness of the doctrine of incorporation and offering praise and criticism from an originalist perspective for the Court's decisions in the areas of criminal procedure, federalism, and religion.

These remarks precipitated an intense popular and scholarly debate as well as critical responses from the Court by Justice William Brennan, who dismissed originalism as "arrogance cloaked as humility" and Justice John Paul Stevens, who noted the inherent difficulties in discerning the original intent of the framers of the Constitution and specifically attempted to rebut Meese's arguments regarding incorporation.[63] These unprecedented inter-branch exchanges have been recognized as "the most direct constitutional debate between the executive branch and the Court since the New Deal," one that created a platform for originalist scholars and compelled members of the liberal legal network to publicly contend with their arguments.[64]

Although Meese's speech to the American Bar Association represented the most visible aspect of the Reagan administration's campaign for a jurisprudence of original intention, also of significance were Meese's subsequent efforts to engage the legal marketplace of ideas directly. This took the form of a series of law review articles arguing in favor of originalism that were published in the immediate aftermath of the speech and were intended to fuel the debate that the speech had precipitated.[65] In these articles, Meese expanded upon the scope of his speech to the American Bar Association, discussing the specific implications for the separation of powers of a jurisprudence of original intention and criticizing Congress for failing to "respect executive prerogatives in regards to the conduct of foreign policy, the appointment of public officials, and those other areas of government authority assigned to the president."[66] The Reagan administration also formally articulated its legal agenda through a number of publications issued by the Department of Justice's Office of Legal Policy. These most prominently included *Original Meaning Jurisprudence: A Sourcebook* and *The Constitution in the Year 2000: Choices Ahead in Constitutional Interpretation*.[67] These publications excoriate the courts for "no longer interpreting our basic charter as ratified" and "usurp[ing] powers not given to them by the people" and declared the administration's support for the proposition that "the founders did not intend future courts to infuse their words with meaning, but to discover and apply the meaning as originally understood."[68] As Teles illustrates, the ultimate success of these efforts in helping to mainstream originalism and mobilize conservatives represents a paradigmatic example of the power of "transformative bureaucracy" to bridge the gap between political-electoral regimes and their activist bases.[69]

The significance of this campaign was underscored by the second major external shock that forced the originalist perspective into constitutional debates: the Reagan administration's subsequent nomination of Robert Bork to the Supreme Court. By nominating the author of "Neutral Principles and Some 1st Amendment Problems," one of the seminal works of originalist scholarship, and of several noteworthy opinions as a federal judge that incorporated originalist arguments, the Reagan administration signaled that its call for a jurisprudence of original intention was not mere rhetoric. Indeed, the Bork nomination has been characterized by Horwitz and others as a "critical moment in constitutional history" on par with the Supreme Court's decision in *Brown v. Board of Education* as it focused the general public's attention upon previously esoteric debates regarding constitutional interpretation.[70] A reflection of the unprecedented level of public interest generated by the Bork nomination was the fact that the Bork hearings were the first Supreme Court confirmation hearings to be televised live and were viewed in whole or in part by nearly 60% of Americans.[71] This public fascination was also the result of the vigorous mobilization against the nomination by a plethora of liberal interest groups. With nearly 150 organized interests taking some action on the nomination, which included several memorable television advertisements, the level of interest group participation was more than three times that of any previous Supreme Court nomination.[72] The galvanizing effect of the Bork nomination can also be attributed to the vitriolic reactions to Bork and to his judicial philosophy by prominent political figures such as Senator Edward Kennedy, who memorably claimed that in Robert Bork's America "women would be forced into back-alley abortions, blacks would sit at segregated lunch counters, rogue police could break down citizens' doors in midnight raids, school children could not be taught about evolution, [and] writers and artists could be censored at the whim of the government."[73] Given that this counter-mobilization led to the Senate's eventual rejection of Bork and the resulting failure of the Reagan administration to change the Supreme Court's ideological balance of power, many have concluded that insofar as the nomination represented a constitutional moment, it was a "failed constitutional moment."[74] Indeed, the fact that nearly 40% of active law professors signed their names to letters to the Senate opposing Bork's confirmation illustrated the continued vitality of the liberal legal network and its apparent imperviousness to the significant changes in the national political environment that had occurred.[75]

However, as O'Neill notes, "the very fact of the Bork nomination and the lengths to which his opponents went to defeat him showed that originalism had changed the climate of American constitutional law."[76] Indeed, Bork's perceived extremism has been credited with shifting the constitutional spectrum to the right and causing jurists such as Antonin Scalia, who share much of Bork's judicial philosophy and would previously have been considered extremists, to be viewed as well within the mainstream.[77] Indeed, it is Scalia, with his long and influential tenure on the Supreme Court and his outspoken role in constitutional debates, who has likely done the most to legitimate originalism as an interpretive philosophy.[78] Moreover, despite the fact that the Reagan administration's campaign for a jurisprudence of original intention failed to persuade the Senate, it succeeded, as Collins and Skover conclude, in causing the "the liberal style of 'judicial activism'...to be seen in a new and more critical light."[79] In particular, by placing the legal liberals opposing it in the position of arguing against the authoritativeness of the text and original meaning of the Constitution and against the sovereignty of popular majorities, this campaign framed the debate in a manner that exposed the weaknesses of legal liberalism.

LEGITIMATING ORIGINALISM

The impact of the Reagan administration's embrace of originalism is also evident in the manner in which it fundamentally changed the dynamics of Supreme Court confirmation hearings, with originalism emerging from obscurity to become a major topic of exchanges between senators and nominees. The extent to which originalism did not figure prominently in constitutional discourse prior to Attorney General Meese's call for a jurisprudence of original intention can be gleaned by contrasting the hearings on the respective nominations of John Paul Stevens and Sandra Day O'Connor with the subsequent hearings on the respective nominations of William Rehnquist, Antonin Scalia, Anthony Kennedy, and David Souter. The hearing transcripts were searched for questions by senators that related to the role that the original intent or original meaning of constitutional provisions should play in their interpretation as well as for questions by senators that related to the nominee's understanding of the original intent or original meaning of specific constitutional provisions. This search revealed that questioning along these lines was virtually non-existent in the Stevens and O'Connor hearings (see Figure 2.2). Other than a single question posed by Senator John Tunney regarding the relevance of historical evidence to construing the 8th Amendment's prohibition against cruel and unusual punishment and a single question posed by Senator Robert Byrd regarding whether the Constitution is a living document, discussion of originalism was absent from the Stevens hearings. Similarly, other than a brief exchange with Senator Orrin Hatch in which the nominee was asked about how she would resolve conflicts between original meaning and precedent and about her view of whether the doctrine of incorporation is consistent with the original intent of the framers of the 14th Amendment, originalism also did not factor into the Senate Judiciary Committee's questioning of Sandra Day O'Connor.

Figure 2.2: Originalism in Supreme Court Confirmation Hearings, 1975-90

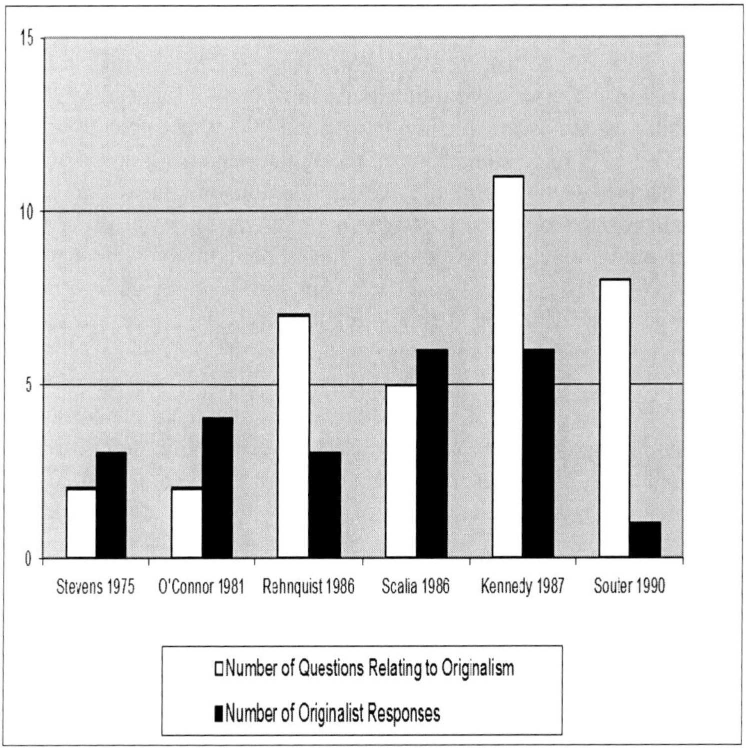

This would change subsequent to Meese's speech to the American Bar Association, with the probing of nominees' views regarding originalism suddenly becoming a prominent theme of Supreme Court confirmation hearings. Moreover, such probing would not be limited to nominees who had previously embraced originalism in their public statements or publications. Thus, not only William Rehnquist, who had published a prominent critique of the concept of a living Constitution, and Antonin Scalia, who had delivered a number of speeches endorsing a jurisprudence of original meaning, but also Anthony Kennedy and David Souter, neither of whom had any "paper trail" linking them to originalism, were subjected to extensive questioning regarding the role of original intent and original meaning in constitutional interpretation.

Most importantly, this questioning also revealed the extent to which the Reagan administration's embrace of originalism quickly migrated to congressional Republicans. Whereas most Republican senators had exhibited no interest in originalism during the Stevens and O'Connor hearings, in subsequent confirmation hearings they would engage nominees in discussions of the original meanings of a broad range of constitutional provisions including Article I §7's Presentment Clause, Article III §2's Exceptions Clause, the 9th Amendment, and the 14th Amendment. Conversely, the Reagan administration's embrace of originalism also led Democratic senators to engage in extensive efforts to draw out nominees' views on the subject, particularly in areas of the law in which Supreme Court precedent is at odds with original meaning. Thus, while the Bork nomination has widely been considered the "trial of originalism" and a turning point in the conduct of Supreme Court confirmation hearings, these data indicate that originalism was already a subject of considerable salience for members of the Senate Judiciary Committee following Meese's speech to the American Bar Association.[80] Moreover, as other analyses of Supreme Court confirmation hearings have demonstrated that the percentage of questions asked that relate to constitutional issues has remained constant since the early 1970s, it can be concluded that the increased incidence of questions relating to originalism represents a specific increase in the salience of originalism rather than an increase in the salience of constitutional issues more generally.[81]

However, while originalism began to feature conspicuously in the Senate Judiciary Committee's questioning of Supreme Court nominees after Meese's call for a jurisprudence of original intention, the extent to which the nominees espoused originalism in their responses would continue to vary considerably. The hearing transcripts were also searched for responses by nominees that positively mentioned original intent or original meaning as sources of constitutional jurisprudence or that drew upon the original intent or original meaning of constitutional provisions in answering questions regarding their interpretation. This search revealed that the greater prominence of originalism in constitutional discourse did not necessarily make nominees more likely to invoke original intent and original meaning in their confirmation hearings. Instead, nominees' responses largely mirrored the ideological tenor of their subsequent jurisprudence as members of the Supreme Court, with John Paul Stevens (who would establish a moderately conservative record early in his tenure on the Court before becoming progressively more liberal over time), Sandra Day O'Connor, William Rehnquist, Antonin Scalia, and Anthony Kennedy each making several references to original intent or original meaning as bases for their jurisprudence while David Souter made only a single indirect reference (conceding that the implicit acceptance of the death penalty by the framers of the Bill of Rights would make it difficult to declare capital punishment cruel and unusual per se).

While the sudden prominence of originalism in Supreme Court confirmation hearings is suggestive, the strongest evidence of the critical role that the Reagan administration's embrace of originalism played in transforming originalism into a mainstream constitutional theory comes from the legal marketplace of ideas. In order to measure the timing and magnitude of the penetration of originalist scholarship into the legal marketplace of ideas, an analysis was conducted of the number of originalist publications and the number of publications critiquing originalism appearing in the 15 most influential law reviews over a ten-year period bracketing the Reagan administration's 1985 call for a jurisprudence of original intention.

Originalist publications were broadly defined as publications making constitutional arguments grounded either in original intent or in original meaning. Thus, publications were coded as originalist if they include significant historical analysis of what constitutional language meant to those who drafted and ratified it, such as McConnell's article contending that "the framers adopted the terminology 'free exercise of religion' to ensure protection for religiously motivated conduct and to make clear the protection would not extend to secular claims of conscience" or significant historical analysis of what the ordinary meaning of constitutional language was at the time of its adoption, such as Epstein's article contending that in 18th century America there were "general and widely shared conceptions of government and contract" that give meaning to the Contracts Clause.[82] This coding protocol excluded publications that merely invoke the name of the framers in a cursory fashion without elaboration. It also limited its definition of originalist publications to those that frame their historical evidence as having contemporary relevance to the constitutional question being analyzed and excluded those that present historical evidence merely a starting point or as something that is merely of historical interest. Thus, publications coded as originalist generally include some statement of contemporary relevance, such as Kmiec's statement that "the concept of property as understood...by the framers has not disintegrated" or Schnapper's statement that "the legislative history of the 14th Amendment is not only relevant to but dispositive of the legal dispute over the constitutional standards applicable to race-conscious affirmative action plans."[83] Originalist publications also include publications making general normative arguments in favor of originalism as the proper method of constitutional interpretation, such as Graglia's argument that "our system of government by lawyer kings in judicial robes...is indefensible in the American context" and that "to interpret the Constitution simply means to determine the intent of its framers."[84]

Publications that directly critique originalism fell primarily into three categories. The first of these included publications that critique originalism on practical grounds by arguing that identifying the original meaning of constitutional language and consistently applying it to contemporary cases and controversies is impossible, such as Chemerinsky's book review arguing that the framers of the Constitution "could not possibly write a document capable of governing future generations facing problems they could never begin to imagine."[85] The second of these included publications that critique originalism on historical grounds by arguing that an originalist jurisprudence would actually be inconsistent with the framers' intent, such as Powell's article contending that "the framers themselves did not believe such an interpretive strategy to be appropriate."[86] Finally, the third of these included publications that critique originalism on normative grounds, such as Seidman's article rejecting the idea of interpreting the Constitution in light of "what a small group of elite white males thought 200 years ago."[87]

A total of 2,107 articles, book reviews, comments, and notes discussing constitutional issues and/or interpretation were published in these law reviews during the time period analyzed. A total of 118 of these publications were coded as originalist and a total of 65 of these publications were coded as counter-originalist. The annual numbers of originalist and counter-originalist publications are expressed as percentages of the total number of articles, book reviews, comments, and notes appearing each year in these law reviews that discuss constitutional issues and/or constitutional interpretation. It was anticipated that a significant increase in the number of originalist publications would follow closely on the heels of Meese's speech to the American Bar Association and subsequent efforts to promote originalism and that this increase would set the stage for a continuous increase in the amount of originalist scholarship over the course of the remainder of the 1980s and the early 1990s as originalism came to be viewed as mainstream constitutional theory. Conversely, it was anticipated that the number of publications critiquing originalism would also increase significantly in the immediate aftermath of the Reagan administration's campaign for a jurisprudence of original intention as legal liberals rose to the challenge of rebutting Meese's arguments and combating the growing influence of originalism in the legal marketplace of ideas. However, it was also anticipated that the number of such critiques would subsequently decline as originalism found broader acceptance. Given the dynamics of the law review editorial process, it was anticipated that the effects of these critical events on the legal marketplace of ideas would begin to materialize within one to two years of their occurrence.

The results (see Figure 2.3) closely correspond to expectations and indicate that that the Reagan administration signaling its embrace of originalism was critical in granting originalist scholarship increased entrée into elite law reviews. This is reflected in the fact that the proportion of originalist publications appearing in the selected law reviews nearly doubled relative to its previous highpoint over the course of the last four years of the time series. Arguably of equal importance is the fact that the results also indicate that these political developments compelled legal liberals to take originalism more seriously as a competing constitutional theory and to attempt to rebut originalist arguments that they had previously ignored. This is reflected in the fact that the number of publications critiquing originalism experienced a similar upsurge in the wake of Meese's speech to the American Bar Association and the Bork nomination (see Figure 2.4). Nonetheless, it is also important to note that the data also indicate the continued vitality of the liberal legal network insofar as, despite the tremendous growth that it experienced, the proportion of originalist publications appearing in elite law reviews barely exceeded ten percent of the publications discussing constitutional issues and/or interpretation at its maximum. This continued vitality is also indicated by the fact that, contrary to expectations, the number of publications critiquing originalism showed no signs of decline in the final years of the time series. This may reflect the partial and protracted nature of the realignment that gave rise to the New Right regime and the regime's lack of political-electoral dominance relative to previous regimes, a lack of dominance that limited its ability to reconstruct the courts, legal institutions, and intellectual climate of its time.

Figure 2.3: Originalist Publications Appearing in the 15 most Influential Law Reviews, 1980-90

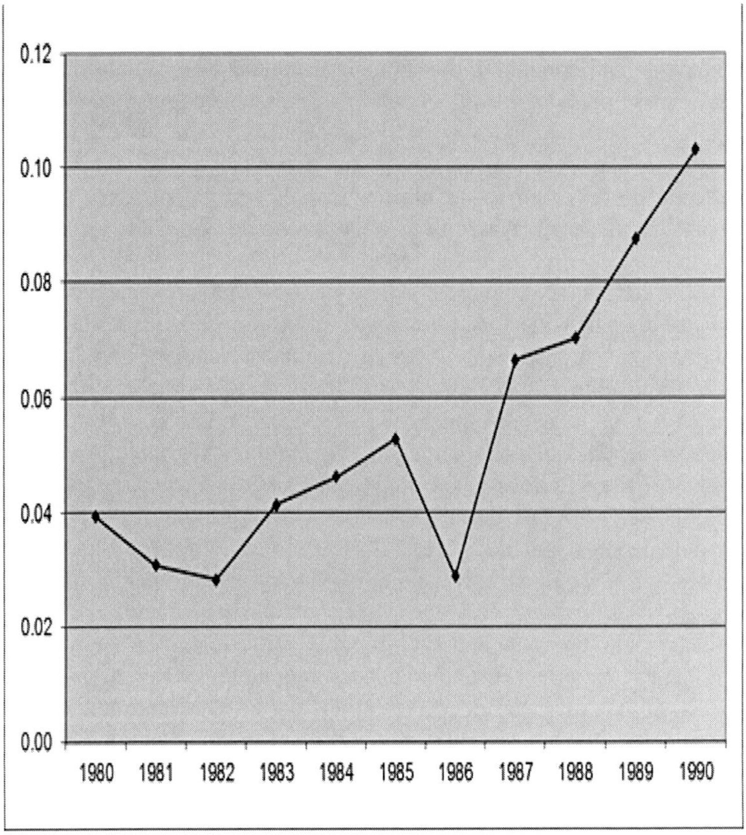

Figure 2.4: Publications Critiquing Originalism Appearing in the 15 most Influential Law Reviews, 1980-90

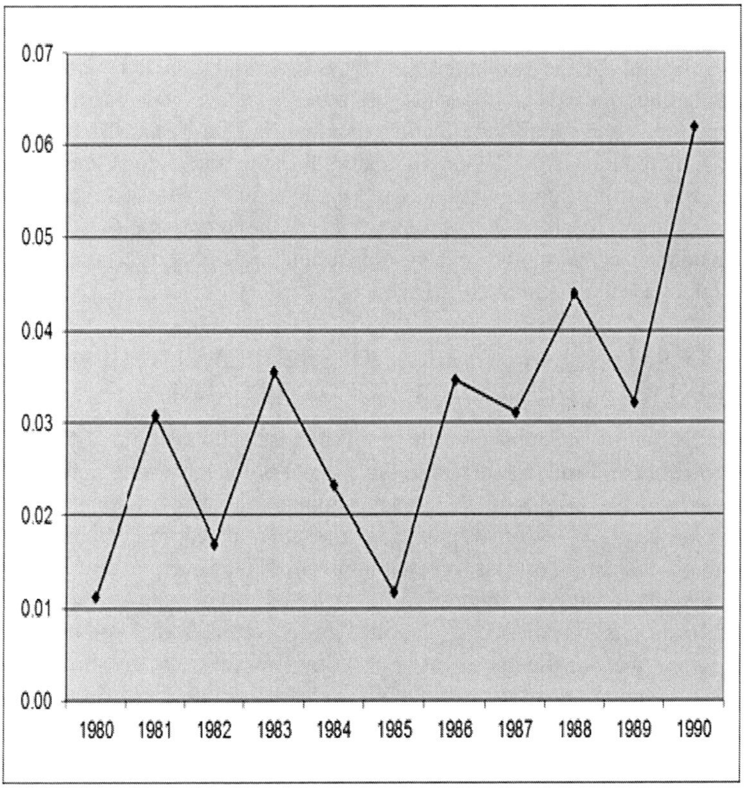

The results also indicate a relatively less important role for support structures for legal mobilization such as the Federalist Society in opening the legal marketplace of ideas to originalist scholarship. For example, comparison of the data presented by Teles regarding the growth of the Federalist Society with the analysis of originalist scholarship in elite law reviews reveals strikingly different patterns of growth. Whereas the number of both law student and lawyer chapters of the Federalist Society grew gradually at a constant rate throughout the 1980s, the growth in the amount of originalist scholarship in elite law reviews was far more abrupt, with the number of originalist publications appearing in these publications fluctuating within a relatively narrow range for several years prior to increasing significantly between 1987 and 1990.[88] Similarly, there is also little correlation between the rate of growth in the amount of originalist scholarship in elite law reviews and the rate of growth in the total membership of the Federalist Society, which was also fairly constant throughout the 1980s.[89] Most importantly, there was virtually no increase in the number of faculty members of the Federalist Society over the course of the 1980s, indicating that the tremendous growth in the amount of originalist scholarship in elite law reviews that occurred during these years was not the result of the professional networks created by conservative legal mobilization increasing the number of originalist scholars in the legal academy.[90]

UNDERSTANDING THE RELATIONSHIP BETWEEN THE NEW RIGHT REGIME AND THE RISE OF ORIGINALISM

While the tremendous growth in originalist scholarship indicates a significant and sudden change in the climate of the legal marketplace of ideas with its origins in the Reagan administration's campaign for a jurisprudence of original intention, the specific causal mechanisms linking the two are less readily apparent. However, a number of possibilities suggest themselves. As has been noted, the legal profession is responsive to realities of power and the embrace of theories that challenge legal orthodoxy by those in positions of institutional authority has frequently helped legitimate those theories. Thus, it is likely that the Reagan administration making originalism the centerpiece of its legal agenda made elite law reviews less able to dismiss originalist perspectives on the law as fringe perspectives and more willing to publish originalist scholarship. Indeed, a number of former Reagan administration officials have identified this as the real purpose of Meese's speeches and articles. According to former Assistant Attorney General Terry Eastland, these speeches and articles were "not necessarily calculated to change anyone's mind…[b]ut rather…to make conservative jurisprudence intellectually respectable again."[91] In addition to conferring greater respectability upon originalist scholarship, the Reagan administration's embrace of originalism also gave such scholarship a newfound salience that made it more likely to appear in elite law reviews. Specifically, given the intense public and scholarly interest generated by the debate between

Meese and Justice Brennan, it is likely that a desire to capitalize upon this interest also made elite law reviews more open to originalist scholarship. Indeed, a number of elite law reviews would attempt to capitalize upon the interest generated by the Meese-Brennan debate by publishing similar exchanges of their own. For example, Cornell Law Review, which had published a mere two pieces of originalist scholarship over the course of the previous decade, would in 1988 publish in its entirety a Federalist Society symposium featuring an exchange between prominent originalists and prominent critics of originalism. Moreover, it is likely that the Reagan administration's campaign for a jurisprudence of original intention also opened the legal marketplace of ideas to originalist scholarship insofar as it sent a powerful signal regarding the type of constitutional argument that would be likely to persuade courts in the future. In particular, by indicating its intent to place originalists on the bench, the Reagan administration increased the practical relevance of constitutional arguments rooted in history. Thus, it is likely that legal scholars responded to this signal by becoming more prone to incorporate such arguments into their scholarship.

The extent to which this is the case is evident in the fact that Meese's speech to the American Bar Association quickly spawned a number of efforts to "harmonize progressive jurisprudence with history."[92] Perhaps the most prominent and illuminating of these attempts by legal liberals to meet originalism on its own terms is Curtis's *No State Shall Abridge: The 14th Amendment and the Bill of Rights*.[93] *No State Shall Abridge* generated widespread interest upon its release insofar as it represented the first piece of scholarship that rebutted on historical grounds Meese's assertions regarding the framers' intent. In particular, in an effort to counter originalist critiques of the doctrine of incorporation, *No State Shall Abridge* marshals historical evidence from the congressional debates on the passage of the 14th Amendment to construct an originalist rationale for the doctrine. This despite the fact that Curtis expresses a number of reservations regarding originalism, in particular the need to consider sources other than original intention in interpreting the Constitution and the indeterminacy of the historical record. Nonetheless, Curtis urges his fellow progressive legal scholars to embrace history because "history provides…legitimacy" and a "tradition against which…calls to restrict individual liberty may be tested," a statement that illustrates the change in the terms of constitutional debates that was unfolding at the time.[94]

Strategic uses of historically based arguments were also common in the law reviews in the wake of the Reagan administration's embrace of originalism. For example, Morais's "Sex Discrimination and the 14th Amendment: Lost History," which presents historical evidence that the framers of the 14th Amendment contemplated the Due Process, Equal Protection, and Privileges and Immunities clauses serving as bases for sex discrimination claims, also exemplifies this broader pattern of many legal liberals responding to originalism's rise to prominence by adopting its methodology.[95] Like Curtis a reluctant originalist, Morais explicitly frames her historical evidence as a safeguard against the possibility that courts may one day be persuaded that the original intention of the 14th Amendment should preclude its application to sex discrimination cases. Noting that the modern consensus in favor of applying heightened scrutiny to sex discrimination under the 14th Amendment had for the first time in years been "challenged in public debate" by Meese and other proponents of originalism, Morais argues that history must be used to "reinforce the consensus view."[96] That originalist arguments could be and increasingly were used to advance liberal ends is also illustrated by the renewal of interest in the egalitarian ideals of the Radical Republican authors of the Reconstruction Amendments. Articles in elite law reviews embodying this trend include, for example, Schnapper's "Affirmative Action and the Legislative History of the 14th Amendment," which argues that the framers of the 14th Amendment's contemporaneous support for race-based programs benefiting former slaves establishes the constitutionality of affirmative action programs, and Vander Velde's "The Labor Vision of the 13th Amendment," which argues that the framers of the 13th Amendment intended for the amendment to not only end slavery but also to protect the rights of workers.[97]

The degree to which the Reagan administration's embrace of originalism changed the climate of the legal marketplace of ideas is also manifest in the change in the legal academy's response to the work of prominent originalist scholars. Perhaps the most important of these scholars is Raoul Berger, whose seminal work has been credited with "profoundly…chang[ing] the assumptions and questions of modern constitutional law scholarship."[98] In contrast to the well known conservative politics of other originalists, Berger's liberal credentials as a former official in Franklin Roosevelt's Department of Justice and self-professed member of the "moderate left of the Democratic Party" made it more difficult for critics to dismiss his scholarship as ideologically motivated.[99] Indeed, one of Berger's first applications of an originalist argument to challenge existing practice and jurisprudence, *Executive Privilege: A Constitutional Myth*, was widely praised and cited by the political left insofar as it rebutted a number of constitutional arguments made by Richard Nixon during the Watergate scandal.[100] Similarly, Berger's first book, *Congress v. The Supreme Court*, had also drawn praise from legal liberals insofar as it defends the practice of judicial review, arguing that the practice was within the original intent of the framers of the Constitution and that congressional efforts to curtail it by withdrawing jurisdiction from federal courts under Article III §2's Exceptions Clause were not.[101] However, Berger would draw the ire of legal liberals with his publication of *Government by Judiciary: The Transformation of the 14th Amendment*, which investigates the original meaning of the 14th Amendment. Berger's argument that the Due Process, Equal Protection, and Privileges and Immunities clauses were drafted for the sole purpose of guaranteeing African Americans the basic rights of citizenship and that therefore *Brown v. Board of Education* and the line of cases incorporating most of the Bill of Rights were incorrectly decided provoked an outpouring of critical commentary from legal liberals. While Berger's later scholarship would be characterized by the same uncompromising originalism, the reception that it was accorded by other legal scholars evolved noticeably over time.

Examining reviews of *Government by Judiciary* and of Berger's two subsequent books, *Death Penalties: The Supreme Court's Obstacle Course* and *Federalism: The Founders' Design*, published in the 15 law reviews that formed the sample for the analysis of originalist and counter-originalist scholarship, this evolution was apparent. On the one hand, the nine reviews of *Government by Judiciary* and *Death Penalties* appearing in these publications are occasionally willing to praise Berger's historical scholarship and even to accept the veracity of some of his conclusions regarding the original meanings of the constitutional provisions that the two works analyze. For example, Bridwell lauds Berger's "well researched and provoking attempt to deal with…important constitutional themes" while Perry concedes that

Berger's history of the 14th Amendment is "substantially accurate."[102] However, on the other hand, not a single one is willing to accept these original meanings as determinative of the contemporary meanings of the 8th and 14th Amendments and endorse originalism as a method of constitutional interpretation. Instead, all share to varying degrees Murphy's view that "the practical results of...reliance on original intent are...disastrous and...can hardly have been intended by framers who were intelligent and patriotic."[103] In contrast, the response to *Federalism*, which appeared subsequent to the launch of the Reagan administration's campaign for a jurisprudence of original intent at a time when originalist scholarship was finding increased acceptance in elite law reviews, was more balanced. While the four reviews of *Federalism* include two strong critiques of originalism by Balkin and Powell, these were accompanied by two generally favorable reviews that defended Berger not only as a historian but also as a constitutional scholar.[104] For example, McConnell praises Berger as "stand[ing] for the honorable tradition that a scholar must put aside his own social and economic predilections and look only to original sources in seeking the meaning of the...Constitution" while a book note in the Harvard Law Review concludes that Federalism "establish[es] firm support for...Berger's controversial contentions."[105]

This trend is further illustrated by the legal academy's response to Robert Bork's *The Tempting of America: The Political Seduction of the Law*, which given Bork's notoriety has undoubtedly been the most widely read and reviewed work written from an originalist perspective.[106] Although the eight negative reviews of *The Tempting of America* published in elite law reviews significantly outnumbered the two positive reviews, the negative responses to Bork's case for originalism were as much a product of the book's harsh tone and its indictment of the legal academy as they were a product of the merits of its arguments regarding constitutional interpretation. Indeed, what is most noteworthy about the negative academic response to *The Tempting of America* is the fact that, in contrast to the negative academic response to earlier originalist scholarship, it included the voices of a number of scholars willing to defend originalism in principle. Thus, for example, although Carter condemns the tone of *The Tempting of America* as "vengeful" and "relentlessly partisan," he is willing to commend originalism as a constitutional theory "very much within the mainstream of contemporary constitutional debate" that rests on the "sensible premise that judges must be bound to something relatively concrete."[107] Similarly, although Denniston finds Bork's "dyspeptic" and "ill-humored" attacks against his critics to be regrettable, he characterizes originalism as a "purely respectable constitutional theory" that "ought to be some part of every judge's machinery of constitutional interpretation."[108] The fact that legal scholars otherwise critical of Bork's approach to constitutional interpretation felt compelled to recognize originalism as a legitimate constitutional theory worthy of serious consideration indicates a sea change, one that is consistent with broader trends in the legal marketplace of ideas that saw originalist scholarship gain newfound acceptance.

This newfound acceptance of conservative legal theory is also indicative of the New Right regime's broader entrenchment in the legal profession, an entrenchment that allowed the regime to overcome its judicial supply-side problem. The waning of the supply-side problem is reflected in Republican presidents' increasing success over time in appointing Supreme Court justices committed to their conservative constitutional vision. This success may be attributed not only to the emergence of conservative legal professional organizations such as the Federalist Society, which provided a critical support structure for judicial selection by identifying and grooming reliably conservative prospective nominees, but also to generational replacement. In particular, the historical context in which jurists come of age has been recognized as a significant influence upon their conception of the law and their approach to its interpretation.[109] The lawyers of the older generation from which judicial nominees were drawn early in the New Right regime received their legal training during the ascendancy of legal realism in the 1930s and 40s and of the Warren Court in the 1950s and 60s. These lawyers also largely made their subsequent careers during a period in which the legal profession was being transformed into a liberal institution, one in which distinctly liberal understandings of the law that are vigorously contested today were considered "'good professional practice,' 'standard operating procedure,' 'the public interest,' [and] 'conventional wisdom.'"[110] In contrast, the younger generation of lawyers from which more recent judicial nominees have been drawn received its legal training during the 1970s and 80s, when the hegemony of the legal ideologies that pervaded the academy during these earlier periods was beginning to be challenged. More importantly, these lawyers largely made their subsequent careers during a period when legal liberalism was no longer "strangely uncontroversial" in the profession and its "conceal[ment of] normative choice in technical garb" had become more apparent.[111]

In order to measure how this generational change has produced change in the ideology of Supreme Court appointees over the course of the New Right regime, measures of the ideology of each justice appointed since the election of Richard Nixon were calculated using Martin and Quinn's estimations of each justice's ideal point in ideological space for each term. New estimations have been added each term through 2013 and are available on the Supreme Court Database. Each justice's estimations were averaged to produce a composite measure of that justice's record during their tenure on the Court (see Table 2.2). Lower scores indicate a more liberal record while higher scores indicate a more conservative record. The results illustrate the depth of the supply-side problem that Republican presidents initially faced when attempting to select conservative Supreme Court nominees from a legal profession permeated by legal liberalism. While Warren Burger, William Rehnquist, Antonin Scalia, and Clarence Thomas established strongly conservative records that pleased the presidents that nominated them, their efforts to move the Court in a direction consistent with the New Right regime's constitutional vision were undermined by the concurrent appointments of Harry Blackmun, John Paul Stevens, and David Souter, who despite having been appointed by Republican presidents established records as liberal as those of any of the Democratic appointees with whom they served. Moreover, while Lewis Powell, Sandra Day O'Connor, and Anthony Kennedy established moderately conservative records, each would be a source of disappointment for conservatives by regularly voting with the Court's liberal bloc in important cases. For example, Powell provided the decisive fifth vote in a number of decisions that displeased conservatives, voting to affirm the constitutionality of affirmative action programs in *Regents of the University of California v. Bakke* and to affirm *Roe v. Wade* in *Thornburgh v. American College of Obstetricians and Gynecologists*. Similarly, O'Connor and Kennedy also consistently voted in favor of affirming *Roe v. Wade* and broke with the Court's conservative bloc in a host of other landmark cases involving issues such as capital punishment, privacy, and religion.

Table 2.2: Supreme Court Appointments during the New Right Regime

Name	*Appointed*	*President*	*Ideology*	*Born*	*Admitted to Bar*
Warren Burger	1969	Nixon	1.85	1907	1931
Harry Blackmun	1970	Nixon	–0.12	1908	1932
Lewis Powell	1972	Nixon	0.93	1907	1931
William Rehnquist	1972	Nixon	2.86	1924	1952
John Paul Stevens	1975	Ford	–1.48	1920	1947
Sandra Day O'Connor	1981	Reagan	0.90	1930	1952
Antonin Scalia	1986	Reagan	3.05	1936	1961
Anthony Kennedy	1987	Reagan	1.04	1936	1961
David Souter	1990	G.H.W. Bush	–0.79	1939	1966
Clarence Thomas	1991	G.H.W. Bush	4.43	1948	1974
Ruth Bader Ginsburg	1993	Clinton	–0.80	1933	1959
Stephen Breyer	1994	Clinton	–0.63	1938	1964
John Roberts	2005	G.W. Bush	2.53	1955	1979
Samuel Alito	2006	G.W. Bush	2.94	1950	1975
Sonia Sotomayor	2009	Obama	0.47	1954	1980
Elena Kagan	2010	Obama	0.66	1960	1986

In contrast to the uneven success of Richard Nixon, Gerald Ford, Ronald Reagan, and George H.W. Bush in selecting Supreme Court nominees who shared the New Right regime's constitutional values, both of the justices appointed to the Court by George W. Bush have proven to be reliable conservatives. This success can be attributed in part to the presence of a larger pool of prospective nominees with unambiguous credentials as legal conservatives. Not only were both John Roberts and Samuel Alito prominent members of the Federalist Society, both had also served in the Reagan administration's Department of Justice, with Roberts serving as deputy assistant to Attorney General William French Smith and Alito serving as deputy assistant to Smith's successor Edwin Meese. While this is consistent with a broader pattern of Republican Supreme Court appointees with previous service in Republican presidential administrations (Warren Burger, William Rehnquist, Antonin Scalia, Clarence Thomas, John Roberts, and Samuel Alito) proving to be more reliable conservatives than Republican Supreme Court appointees without such experience (Harry Blackmun, Lewis Powell, Sandra Day O'Connor, Anthony Kennedy, and David Souter), it also indicates the importance of the Federalist Society as a support structure for the conservative legal movement.

It also suggests the importance of the rise of a new generation of lawyers. In particular, Clarence Thomas (a member of Yale Law School's class of 1974), John Roberts (a member of Harvard Law School's class of 1979), and Samuel Alito (a member of Yale Law School's class of 1975) were the first members of the "baby boom" generation appointed to the Court. These justices attended law school during the formative years of the New Right regime, which saw the liberal consensus of the New Deal regime collapse and conservatism gain newfound intellectual respectability. More importantly, these justices attended law school against the backdrop of a powerful political, and to a lesser extent academic, backlash against legal liberalism. Not only was the Republican Party, beginning with Richard Nixon and continuing with subsequent Republican presidents, engaging in increasingly strong rhetorical attacks on the judiciary in general and the Supreme Court in particular, the verities of legal liberalism were beginning to be challenged in the legal academy by scholars such as Robert Bork and Raoul Berger. Moreover, as Graber and Keck explain, the fact that the liberal judicial activism of the Warren Court was a fading memory for these justices by the time that they began their legal careers has contributed to their placing less emphasis than conservatives of prior generations upon judicial restraint and to their being more willing to engage in the sort of conservative judicial activism that a true jurisprudence of original intent would entail.[112]

However, as Graber illustrates, the conservative judicial activism that the new generation of Republican jurists has engaged in has tended to reflect the priorities of certain elements of the New Right coalition while largely paying lip service to the priorities of other elements of the New Right coalition.[113] In particular, these jurists have been far more conservative and far more activist on economic issues than on social issues. This reflects the fact that Republican judicial nominees have invariably been drawn from the ranks of well-educated and affluent Republican elites, who as a group have generally been less conservative on social issues than rank and file Republicans. This divide between Republican legal elites and rank and file Republicans is also evident in the work of conservative legal scholars, most of whom have focused on "writ[ing] bold arguments for judicial activism on behalf of libertarianism" while "hav[ing] little affinity for religious communitarianism."[114] It is therefore not surprising that the Roberts Court has devoted particular attention to cases involving union and economic activity and that it has been markedly more conservative than previous courts in its disposition of such cases.[115] This more activist brand of conservatism in economic activity cases can be traced to the replacement of William Rehnquist and Sandra Day O'Connor by John Roberts and Samuel Alito.

This generational divide is also evident in the records of Antonin Scalia and Clarence Thomas, who despite sharing a strong commitment to originalism have followed markedly different approaches to precedent. As Scalia himself has noted in distinguishing their judicial philosophies, Thomas "doesn't believe in stare decisis, period."[116] Instead, consistent with his stated belief that "the ultimate precedent is the Constitution," Thomas has distinguished himself from his more senior Republican colleagues with his steadfast adherence to the principle that "if a constitutional line of authority is wrong...let's get it right."[117] In contrast, these senior colleagues have generally been reluctant to overturn lines of precedent that have become deeply ingrained into the fabric of constitutional law, even if those lines of precedent are inconsistent with the original meaning of the

Constitution. This more restrained approach was most self-consciously adopted by William Rehnquist, who notably refused to overturn *Miranda v. Arizona* despite his disagreement with the logic underlying the decision, declaring in his majority opinion in *Dickerson v. United States* that stare decisis "carries such persuasive force that we have always required a departure from precedent to be supported by some 'special justification.'"[118]

This approach reflected a distinctive set of historical influences that contributed to the judicial supply-side problem that Republican presidents encountered early in the life cycle of the New Right regime. In particular, Richard Nixon's first three appointments to the Court (Warren Burger, Harry Blackmun, and Lewis Powell) as well as Gerald Ford's sole appointment to the Court (John Paul Stevens) were members of the "greatest generation," which came of age during the Great Depression and served in World War II. With the exception of Stevens, these justices attended law school during the disintegration of the 4th Party System's Republican regime, which saw the laissez faire economic policies and anti-statism that had been associated with this regime discredited. More importantly, the discrediting of these ideologies also discredited the formalist legal ideology that had constitutionalized them and contributed to the meteoric rise of the legal realist movement in the academy. These historical influences left a legacy that made it difficult for justices who were members of this generation to embrace originalism even if they were political conservatives. Not only did the ascendancy of realist conceptions of the law during the Great Depression make them wary of a return to any sort of formalism, the discrediting of the unprecedented activism of the Lochner era Supreme Court and of the doctrine of economic substantive due process that was the basis for this activism meant that these justices often had "difficulty accepting judicial activism, even when the justices were making policy that they supported."[119] Thus, even if they were sympathetic to the political ends that would be advanced by a jurisprudence of original intent, they were unlikely to embrace a jurisprudence that would depart so radically from longstanding precedent and would force the Court into a confrontation with the elected branches of government that would be reminiscent of the Lochner Court's confrontation with Franklin Roosevelt.

Similar historical baggage would also make it difficult for the next generation of Republican appointees to completely embrace the New

Right regime's revolutionary legal agenda. Although these members of the "silent generation" (William Rehnquist and Sandra Day O'Connor) had little personal memory of the Lochner Court, they attended law school during a time in which its legacy continued to shape the zeitgeist, creating an atmosphere hostile to formalism generally and to conservative judicial activism specifically. These were years in which talk of the counter-majoritarian difficulty posed by judicial review dominated academic discourse on constitutional law and the Supreme Court had yet to embark upon the activism of the Warren Court years, remaining firmly under the control of proponents of judicial restraint.[120] Thus, although Rehnquist and O'Connor's willingness to use judicial power to enforce the New Right regime's distinctively conservative form of rights-based constitutionalism was somewhat at odds with the spirit of this period, their unwillingness to use judicial power to nullify the liberal rights-based constitutionalism that had been woven into the constitutional fabric by the Warren Court was wholly consistent with it. For different reasons, the next generation of Republican appointees (Anthony Kennedy, Antonin Scalia, and David Souter), who launched their careers at the height of the Warren Court's activism (and the height of liberalizing trends in the legal profession), were also likely to disappoint the presidents that nominated them. While this generation was capable of producing a Scalia, whose speeches extolling originalism and background as one of the first faculty members of the Federalist Society left little doubt that he would be a consistently conservative jurist, it more often produced Kennedys and Souters, jurists who to varying degrees embraced the liberal constitutionalism of the Warren Court despite their Republican affiliations.

The more consistent conservatism of George W. Bush's Supreme Court appointees relative to those of previous Republican presidents can also be attributed to the unique political dynamics of the New Right regime, particularly its initial inability to translate its success in presidential elections into congressional majorities. As a result of this inability, most of the justices appointed by the four Republican presidents who preceded George W. Bush faced confirmation in Senates with Democratic majorities. Of the ten justices appointed by these presidents, eight were confirmed by Democratic-controlled Senates while only two (Sandra Day O'Connor and Antonin Scalia) were confirmed by Republican-controlled Senates. This undoubtedly tempered those presidents' choices of nominees and resulted in

Democratic-controlled Senates rejecting not only the Bork nomination but also Richard Nixon's nominations of Clement Haynsworth and Harrold Carswell. However, although the fact that Ronald Reagan was denied the opportunity to place Robert Bork on the Court and forced to turn to Anthony Kennedy as a replacement clearly represented a lost opportunity for the New Right regime to move the Court to the right, it is less clear whether the successive defeats of the Haynsworth and Carswell nominations and the subsequent appointment of Harry Blackmun had much effect on the Court's ideological balance. This is particularly the case with the Haynsworth nomination given that Haynsworth's record as a judge on the 4th Circuit Court of Appeals has been retrospectively described as "moderate" and "close in outlook to John Paul Stevens."[121] Thus, had Haynsworth been confirmed his jurisprudence, like Blackmun's, would likely have been markedly less conservative than was anticipated at the time of his nomination and illustrated the depth of the liberal consensus among elite lawyers of his generation.

That the conservative legal movement has changed the ideological balance of power within the legal profession is indicated not only by the waning of the New Right regime's supply-side problem but also by the potential emergence of one on the Democratic side. In particular, it is noteworthy that both of the justices appointed to the Court by Barack Obama, who are the youngest and third youngest members of the Court, have established relatively centrist records that are less liberal than those of the justices appointed by Bill Clinton, both of whom came of age during the Warren Court years. This despite Sonia Sotomayor and Elena Kagan having been appointed by a more liberal president and in a political environment that placed fewer constraints upon that president's choice of nominees. While the brevity of Sotomayor and Kagan's tenures on the Court make it difficult to draw any definitive conclusions, this may be symptomatic of the general shift of the constitutional spectrum to the right. It may also be indicative of Barack Obama's place in political time. While some had speculated early in his presidency that Obama would be a reconstructive president whose reconstruction of the political order would include transformative appointments of "decidedly liberal, pro-regulatory activist[s]" who would be well to the left of Bill Clinton's Supreme Court appointees, this appears not to be the case.[122]

CONCLUSIONS

In sum, while Teles concludes that conservative legal mobilization solved the problem of the "lack [of] legitimacy in the highest ranks of the legal academy" that legal theories such as originalism suffered from, examining patterns of change in the legal marketplace of ideas reveals a more complex reality, one that is suggested by Teles's own subsequent case study of the Reagan administration's Department of Justice and its efforts to promote originalism [123] While conservative legal mobilization played a critical role in transforming inchoate conservative hostility to legal liberalism into a coherent originalist critique and in grooming the reliably conservative lawyers needed to implement the New Right regime's legal agenda, it was by itself insufficient to confer greater legitimacy upon conservative legal theory. This would only come when this originalist critique was openly embraced by the Reagan administration, signaling to the legal academy and to the legal profession that originalism was not merely a fringe theory and that it should be taken seriously insofar as it was likely to influence the future development of constitutional law. This indicates the limits of legal mobilization and suggests that while control of political institutions is not a sufficient condition for legal change absent an adequate support structure for legal mobilization, it may be a necessary condition given the ideational entrenchment that otherwise characterizes the legal marketplace of ideas. In order to determine whether this is the case, it is necessary to examine how the rise of other important legal intellectual movements has been intertwined with the rise of new political-electoral regimes.

CHAPTER 3

Legal Realism and the New Deal Regime

INTRODUCTION

"We are all realists now." While statements to this effect have been "made so frequently that it has become a truism to refer to [them] as…truism[s]," they are nonetheless indicative of the transformation in legal thought that is associated with the emergence of the legal realist movement.[1] Challenging the premises of the legal formalism that once permeated legal thought, the legal realist movement has been credited with banishing conceptions of the law as a complete, autonomous, and apolitical system in which judges merely discover rather than make law. Moreover, just as the conservative legal movement's success in renewing interest in history as a source of constitutional meaning came at a time when the Reagan administration was actively promoting originalism, the success of the legal realist movement in changing the terms of legal and constitutional discourse has been widely associated with Franklin Roosevelt's efforts to promote the idea of a living Constitution.[2] In order to better understand the relationship between the rise of the New Deal political-electoral regime and the realist turn in legal thought, this chapter analyzes the temporal relationship between trends in legal education and scholarship, the Roosevelt administration's embrace of legal realism, and the growth in the amount of realist scholarship published in elite law reviews. It finds that while this embrace of legal realism contributed to upsurges in realist scholarship, these upsurges built upon a foundation laid by earlier progressive critiques of legal formalism and by social forces that moved legal education and scholarship in the direction advocated by realists.

THE RISE OF THE NEW DEAL REGIME

The New Deal regime represents one of the most thorough and sustained periods of political and electoral dominance enjoyed by any political party in American history, a period that saw the Democratic

Party dominate American politics to a greater extent than the Republican Party during either the preceding 4th Party System or the subsequent New Right regime (see Table 3.1). Not only did Democratic candidates win seven of the nine presidential elections held between 1932 and 1964, with war hero Dwight Eisenhower the only Republican able to break the Democrats' lock on the presidency, the Democratic Party simultaneously controlled both houses of Congress for 32 of the regime's 36 years. Moreover, the size of the some of the majorities with which it did so had not been seen since Reconstruction and have not been seen since. For example, the 75th Congress, which met from 1937 to 1939 and in which Democrats held 334 seats in the House of Representatives and 76 seats in the Senate, remains the last time that one party has held more than three quarters of the seats in both houses of Congress. Over the life cycle of the New Deal regime, the Democratic Party would hold an average of 260 seats in the House of Representatives and 60 seats in the Senate, averages that made the New Deal regime far more dominant in congressional elections than either the 4th Party System's Republican regime or the New Right regime. The Democratic Party enjoyed a similarly robust advantage in macro-partisanship during the New Deal regime. The percentage of Americans identifying as Democrats steadily increased over the course of the 1930s, 40s, and 50s and peaked in 1964, when more than 50% of Americans identified as Democrats (and only 25% identified as Republicans). Conversely, the percentage of Americans identifying as Republicans never reached 40% at any point during this period.[3]

These numbers illustrate the depth of the "New Deal earthquake" that realigned American politics in the 1930s.[4] As the Great Depression produced a clamor for government action that the conservative Hoover administration proved unwilling to respond to, the Democratic Party under the leadership of Franklin Roosevelt attempted to answer by re-branding itself as a progressive party committed to a more activist state. This re-branding of a party that throughout the 1920s had attempted to accommodate the conservative national mood

Table 3.1: Partisan Control of Political Institutions during the New Deal Regime

Congress (Years)	*House of Representatives (Party Breakdown)*	*Senate (Party Breakdown)*	*Presidency (President)*	*Control*
73rd (1933-1935)	Democratic (313-117-5)	Democratic (59-36-1)	Democratic (F. Roosevelt)	Complete
74th (1935-1937)	Democratic (322-103-7-3)	Democratic (69-25-1-1)	Democratic (F. Roosevelt)	Complete
75th (1937-1939)	Democratic (334-88-8-5)	Democratic (76-16-2-1-1)	Democratic (F. Roosevelt)	Complete
76th (1939-1941)	Democratic (262-169-2-1-1)	Democratic (69-23-2-1-1)	Democratic (F. Roosevelt)	Complete
77th (1941-1943)	Democratic (267-162-3-1-1-1)	Democratic (66-28-1-1)	Democratic (F. Roosevelt)	Complete
78th (1943-1945)	Democratic (222-209-2-1-1)	Democratic (57-38-1)	Democratic (F. Roosevelt)	Complete
79th (1945-1947)	Democratic (242-191-1-1)	Democratic (57-38-1)	Democratic (F. Roosevelt/Truman)	Complete
80th (1947-1949)	Republican (246-188-1)	Republican (51-45)	Democratic (Truman)	Divided
81st (1949-1951)	Democratic (263-171-1)	Democratic (54-42)	Democratic (Truman)	Complete
82nd (1951-1953)	Democratic (235-199-1)	Democratic (49-47)	Democratic (Truman)	Complete
83rd (1953-1955)	Republican (221-213-1)	Republican (48-47-1)	Republican (Eisenhower)	Opposition
84th (1955-1957)	Democratic (232-203)	Democratic (48-47-1)	Republican (Eisenhower)	Divided
85th (1957-1959)	Democratic (234-201)	Democratic (49-47)	Republican (Eisenhower)	Divided
86th (1959-1961)	Democratic (283-153-1)	Democratic (65-35)	Republican (Eisenhower)	Divided
87th (1961-1963)	Democratic (263-174)	Democratic (64-36)	Democratic (Kennedy)	Complete
88th (1963-1965)	Democratic (259-176)	Democratic (66-34)	Democratic (Kennedy/Johnson)	Complete
89th (1965-1967)	Democratic (295-140)	Democratic (68-32)	Democratic (Johnson)	Complete
90th (1967-1969)	Democratic (247-187)	Democratic (64-36)	Democratic (Johnson)	Complete

of the latter years of the 4th Party System produced a dramatic realignment of the electorate. Whereas the partisan alignments of the 4th Party System had, despite the realigning election of 1896, largely continued to reflect the regional cleavages created by the Civil War and Reconstruction, the new partisan alignments that emerged were much more class-based and ideological. Those in the lower economic classes, who tended to be the strongest supporters of using government to combat the Great Depression and provide for social welfare, gravitated toward the Democratic Party while those in the upper economic classes, who tended to favor laissez faire economic policies and a more limited role for government, gravitated toward the Republican Party. This class polarization significantly broadened the Democratic coalition, adding the votes of the urban working class and African Americans to the party's Southern base and increasing the party's support among Catholics and recent immigrant groups. It also provided the Democratic Party with new bases of organizational support as it was during this period that close and enduring ties were established between the party and organized labor.[5]

It was this coalition that propelled Franklin Roosevelt to landslide victories in the 1932 and 1936 presidential elections, elected Democratic supermajorities in Congress, and whose loyalties to the Democratic Party were cemented by the relief provided by the Roosevelt administration's New Deal programs. However, although the Democratic Party would remain the nation's majority party for the duration of the New Deal regime, Democratic control of Congress did not necessarily guarantee a liberal majority in Congress as Democrats, particularly Southern Democrats, who took conservative positions on many issues were always a significant presence in the Democratic caucus. Although Roosevelt attempted to purge the Democratic Party of some of its conservative elements in the 1938 midterm elections by publicly supporting a number of liberal primary challengers against conservative incumbents, this strategy failed as most of these conservative Democrats were reelected and the Republican Party made significant gains.[6] These gains, driven by economic recession and by backlash against Roosevelt's controversial "court-packing" plan, allowed Republicans and conservative Democrats to form an informal "conservative coalition" that would effectively control Congress for the next two decades.[7] This alliance halted any further significant expansion of the New Deal until 1964, when Democrats regained sufficiently large supermajorities in both houses of Congress to pass Medicare, Medicaid, and other parts of Lyndon Johnson's Great Society.

Although the Democratic Party was increasingly divided ideologically, it largely succeeded in maintaining its unity in presidential elections. While he did so with smaller majorities than in his first two elections, Franklin Roosevelt managed to win reelection to unprecedented third and fourth terms in 1940 and 1944, respectively, and his successor Harry Truman was successful in winning election in his own right in 1948 despite low public approval ratings and third party campaigns waged by both disaffected Southern Democrats and disaffected liberal Democrats. However, Democrats were unable to overcome the personal popularity of Dwight Eisenhower, whose notoriety as supreme commander of Allied forces during World War II allowed him to win comfortable victories in the 1952 and 1956 presidential elections. Nonetheless, these were the personal victories of a preemptive president who accepted (and in some areas expanded) the New Deal and did little to build the Republican Party. Although Republicans won majorities in both houses of Congress in 1952 on the coattails of Eisenhower's victory, these majorities were immediately lost in the 1954 midterm elections (just as the congressional majorities that Republicans won in 1946 were also immediately lost after one election) and by the end of Eisenhower's presidency the Democratic Party enjoyed its largest majorities since the New Deal. Without Eisenhower at the top of the ticket there also was a return to the normal dynamics of presidential elections, which heavily favored the Democrats, as John F. Kennedy won a narrow victory in 1960 and Lyndon Johnson won a landslide victory in 1964.

This victory has been called the "high tide of liberalism" and the Great Society programs that it made possible represented the culmination of a long era of liberal reform that began with the progressive movement of the early 20th century.[8] However, it was also in 1964 that the inherent incompatibility of some of the constituencies that comprised the New Deal coalition began to bring about its dissolution. Although Northern liberals and African Americans had long been joined in an uneasy alliance with Southern conservatives by their shared support for the New Deal, the emergence of civil rights as a national issue would make continued coexistence impossible and contribute to the rise of the New Right regime. The first rupture came in 1948, when the successful insertion of a civil rights plank in the Democratic Party platform by Northern liberals led to many Southern Democrats defecting from the party and forming the States' Rights Democratic Party, which ran on a platform of protecting segregation from federal interference and won the electoral votes of four Southern states. When this tactic failed to deny Harry Truman the presidency and force the Democratic Party to moderate its position, most of the Southern Democrats who had left the party quietly returned, as the Republican Party remained equally inhospitable to their views. However, this changed in 1964, when the Republican presidential nominee was Barry Goldwater, who as a member of the Senate had voted against the 1964 Civil Rights Act. Running against the president who had worked tirelessly for the law's passage, Goldwater carried five Southern states, three of which had not voted Republican since Reconstruction and one of which had never before voted Republican. Although occurring against the backdrop of a massive defeat for the Republican Party nationally, this was a watershed moment that marked the transformation of a normally Democratic region into a normally Republican region in presidential elections.[9] This transformation would serve as one of the foundations of the New Right regime that emerged a few years later when backlash against the liberalism of the Democratic Party spread from the South to the North.

LEGAL FORMALISM CONTESTED

Just as the entrenchment of legal liberalism in the legal profession represented an obstacle for the New Right regime to overcome in implementing its legal agenda, the entrenchment of legal formalism in the legal profession had represented an obstacle for the New Deal regime 50 years earlier. Legal formalism was a reflection of the economic conservatism of political and legal elites in a period of class conflict. By erecting a conceptual boundary between private law and public law, formalism created an independent realm of private rights secure from popular pressures for regulation and redistribution.[10] As surveys of trends in American legal education have illustrated, legal formalism was also a product of a deeply rooted legal culture that was inculcated in lawyers and jurists in the law schools.[11] This legal culture had its origins in Christopher Langdell's tenure as the dean of Harvard Law School from 1870 to 1895. Believing that law is a science that can be reduced to sets of general principles providing rules of decision for any fact pattern that may arise, Langdell was the driving force behind Harvard Law School's adoption of the case method. While the case method, and the formalistic approach to the law that it engendered, was controversial at the time of its introduction and met with some initial resistance from the legal profession, it had a number of advantages that eventually led to its adoption by law schools nationwide. As Kalman explains, not only was the case method cost effective insofar as it permitted much higher student to teacher ratios than more traditional modes of legal education, its scientific veneer also dovetailed with the law schools' desire to legitimate law as an academic discipline.[12] Perhaps most importantly, the unparalleled institutional prestige of Harvard Law School ensured that the case method would quickly be copied by other law schools. The formalism of the legal culture of this period was also manifest in the American Law Institute's Restatement of the Law project, which was launched in 1923. This prominent effort to reduce entire fields of the law to a handful of "black letter" principles was the work of a number of Langdell's former students who saw it as the ultimate realization of his vision.[13] However, despite the apparent success of the Restatement of the Law project in systematizing the law, powerful intellectual, legal, and social currents running counter to the formalism it represented were already making themselves felt.

Indeed, although the late 19th and early 20th centuries are generally remembered as a period in which formalism permeated legal discourse, a significant cadre of jurists and scholars had challenged formalism from its inception. Thus, as Horwitz explains, realist critiques of legal formalism were not original but rather represented a "continuation of the progressive attack on the attempt of late 19th century classical legal thought to create a sharp distinction between law and politics and to portray law as neutral, natural, and apolitical."[14] The seminal works in this line of progressive legal scholarship were future Supreme Court Justice Oliver Wendell Holmes's *The Common Law*, widely remembered for its realist maxim that "the life of the law has not been logic, it has been experience," and "The Path of the Law," which further expounds Holmes's pragmatic approach to the law.[15] Holmes's attacks on legal formalism in both his scholarly writings and his judicial opinions would serve as an inspiration for subsequent calls for a sociological jurisprudence by scholars such as Roscoe Pound and Joseph Bingham.

In particular, Pound's critique of "mechanical jurisprudence" and his call for the judges to "adjust…[legal] principles and doctrines to the human conditions they are to govern rather than to assumed first principles" foreshadowed arguments made by legal realists two decades later.[16] The same could be said of Bingham's assertion that the widely held belief that law is a coherent system of rules and principles is "fundamentally erroneous and…a bar to a scientific understanding of…[the] law and its particular problems."[17] Early precursors to the rise of legal realism can also be found in the increasing frequency with which social science was incorporated into legal and constitutional arguments. For instance, the success of the "Brandeis brief," which eschewed reliance upon legal and constitutional theory in favor of reliance upon empirical data, in persuading the Supreme Court of the constitutionality of restrictions on the working hours of women in *Muller v. Oregon* quickly made it a model for arguments in cases involving the health and welfare of classes of individuals.[18]

Nonetheless, there were also important discontinuities between sociological jurisprudence and legal realism. In particular, legal realism can be distinguished from sociological jurisprudence by its more profound skepticism of the neutrality and rationality of the judicial process, a consequence of which was that realists tended to be less court-centered and more interested in achieving legal change through statutory and administrative law than their forebears.[19] In this respect both movements were a reflection of the zeitgeist of the historical period in which they emerged, with sociological jurisprudence reflecting the optimism and faith in human reason and science of the Progressive Era and legal realism reflecting the pessimism and nihilism of the Great Depression.

However, although sociological jurisprudence has consequently often been described as the "jurisprudential analog" to the progressive movement, it would never pervade legal thought and jurisprudence to the extent that legal realism subsequently would.[20] As Stone explains, the proponents of sociological jurisprudence were confronted in their time with a "struggl[e] for intellectual legitimacy in the face of…conceptualism and logicism" that their long term success in changing attitudes toward the law has obscured.[21] Thus, while Holmes' proto-realist jurisprudence was celebrated by progressives and by likeminded scholars such as Pound and Bingham, it usually placed him in the minority during his time on the Court, as his historical reputation as "the great dissenter" indicates.[22] Similarly, despite Pound's authoritative position as the dean of the University of Nebraska College of Law (and later Harvard Law School), his calls for a sociological jurisprudence were initially met with considerable resistance from the legal establishment, with his 1906 speech on the flaws of the American legal thought and jurisprudence "so shock[ing] the conservative leaders at the annual meeting of the American Bar Association that a motion to print and distribute 4,000 copies was withdrawn."[23]

Nonetheless, despite facing opposition in the courts and in the organized legal profession, sociological jurisprudence would gain traction from the embrace of many of its arguments against legal formalism by prominent political actors associated with the progressive movement. Spearheading constitutional changes at the national level that included the federal income tax, the direct election of senators, Prohibition, and women's suffrage as well as numerous reforms at the state and local levels, the progressive movement represented a nationwide reformist impulse that gave rise to powerful factions within both major political parties.[24] Most importantly, as Gillman explains, the progressive movement was defined by its support for the "positive use of public power" and in large part represented a reaction against the laissez faire policies constitutionalized by legal formalism.[25] Consequently, Theodore Roosevelt and other leading progressives frequently attacked the assumptions underlying legal formalism as antiquated in the Industrial Age, with Roosevelt pointedly asserting that "[i]n the present day the limitation of governmental power…means the enslavement of the people by the great corporations."[26] Moreover, this embrace of the use of public power to check growing corporate influence and to protect vulnerable classes from the ills of industrial capitalism also ran counter to formalist distinctions between "legitimate general welfare legislation and illegitimate factional politics," which held such uses of public power to be unconstitutional "class legislation."[27]

These tensions between progressivism and legal formalism often produced even more direct attacks on the judiciary and its institutional power. This was particularly the case in the 1896 presidential election, in which Democratic nominee William Jennings Bryan and his surrogates regularly denounced the Supreme Court as an "instrument of

Republican corporate power."[28] Similar themes were articulated in the 1912 presidential election, in which, for example, Theodore Roosevelt's Progressive Party proposed that judicial decisions declaring statutes unconstitutional be subject to referenda. These themes were also regularly articulated by many of the nation's leading public intellectuals. These most prominently included Herbert Croly, whose 1915 book *Progressive Democracy* attacked the Supreme Court as a negative and counter-majoritarian force in American politics and is credited with coining the phrase "living Constitution," and Walter Weyl, whose 1912 book *The New Democracy* attacked the Court's jurisprudence as emblematic of the excessive individualism of American culture.[29] Such attacks were also staples of national periodicals such as Harper's Weekly and The New Republic, which brought the ideals of the progressive movement to a mass audience.[30]

Thus, although sociological jurisprudence emerged at a time when the Supreme Court was controlled by the formalist majority that delivered decisions such as *Lochner v. New York* and national politics was dominated by the Republican political-electoral regime of the 4th Party System, it was not entirely lacking in institutional support. Indeed, sociological jurisprudence was in the same tradition as efforts by many of the most important political figures of its time, including Presidents Theodore Roosevelt and Woodrow Wilson and three-time Democratic presidential nominee William Jennings Bryan, to construct a "new American state."[31] Nonetheless, although the implicit embrace of sociological jurisprudence by Theodore Roosevelt and other leading Republicans was a reflection of the uneasy coexistence within the Republican coalition of conservative and progressive factions, this coexistence was somewhat less evident in the courts, which were widely perceived as bastions of conservatism at both the federal and state levels.

THE REALIST TURN IN LEGAL THOUGHT

However, the conservatism of American legal culture began to wane as external forces pushed it in the direction advocated by Holmes, Pound, and Bingham. The realist turn in legal thought coincided with a broad trend in the social sciences toward functionalism and behaviorism that also began to unfold early in the 20th century. Anthropologists, economists, psychologists, and other social scientists responded to the tremendous economic and social upheaval of the period by shifting their focus away from abstract models that no longer described reality and toward the actual dynamics of institutions and human behavior. This was also in part a legacy of Darwinism and its subsequent application to the social sciences by prominent sociologists such as William Graham Sumner, which also contributed to this "shift in emphasis away from structure and toward operations."[32] These developments in the social sciences would be closely observed and consciously emulated by legal scholars still aspiring to make their relatively young discipline more "scientific." This desire for more empirical legal scholarship modeled upon the social sciences was manifest in a number of developments in legal education in the 1920s, such as the introduction of academic doctorates in law at a number of elite universities.[33] These doctoral programs were intended to provide graduates with a theoretical understanding of the nature of the law and the legal system not provided by traditional law school curricula that were oriented toward preparing students for bar examinations. This fusion of law and social science dovetailed with the pedagogical aims of the proponents of sociological jurisprudence. Indeed, the initiative to establish an academic doctorate in law at Harvard was led by Roscoe Pound, who viewed it as a "vehicle for spreading his vision of a 'sociological jurisprudence.'"[34]

Another external force that drove the turn toward realism was an increase in legal uncertainty. As Gilmore explains, the traditional assumptions underlying the case law system were proving untenable by the 1920s.[35] In particular, with the number of published decisions increasing exponentially due to the establishment of the National Reporter System in the late 19th century, it became increasingly unrealistic to imagine that case law provides a coherent set of general principles that can be consistently applied to particular fact patterns. As judges were increasingly being forced to choose from among a multitude of relevant but often wildly divergent precedents, formalist conceptions of jurisprudence as a science no longer provided an accurate representation of what judges were actually doing. Perhaps most importantly, lawyers were finding as a result that predicting case outcomes and advising clients accordingly was becoming increasingly difficult. Given this widening gap between "law in books" and "law in action," it was inevitable that legal scholarship would eventually attempt to bridge this gap by highlighting the practical considerations that actually drive judicial behavior. This gap between law in books and law in action was also a product of the evolution of the American legal system in the early 20th century. As law was increasingly codified in statutes and the common law lost much of its traditional importance, "parsing cases and explicating common law rules seemed less useful and less interesting."[36]

The influence of these external forces upon legal thought is evident in critical assessments of the direction of legal scholarship by figures in positions of institutional authority within the legal academy and profession in the 1920s. Perhaps the most prominent of these figures was Herman Oliphant, who served as the president of the Association of American Law Schools from 1927 to 1928. Oliphant's 1927 presidential address to the association's annual meeting has been widely remembered as a landmark "call to action" for legal scholars to "storm the barricades of formalism and to breathe new life and realism into their scholarship."[37] Bemoaning the limitations of legal scholarship's traditional focus upon rules and principles, Oliphant exhorted legal scholars to turn their attention away from the reasons judges give for their decisions and toward the actual bases for those decisions.[38] Given Oliphant's authoritative position, this speech served as a key impetus for the legal realist movement's subsequent rise to prominence. Another voice speaking from a position of authority that lent early credibility to the emerging legal realist movement was United States District Court Judge Joseph Hutcheson. Given his position as a sitting federal judge, Hutcheson's acknowledgement in a prominent 1929 law review article that his decisions were based upon "an intuitive sense of what is right or wrong for that case" and "not by ratiocination" and his call for legal scholarship to devote greater attention to the subjective "processes of mind by which...decisions are reached" were particularly significant.[39]

This growing dissatisfaction with the detachment of legal discourse from reality was exacerbated by the Great Depression, which made formalistic distinctions between the public and private spheres and their idea of the market as "self-regulating and outside government control" appear ever more anachronistic.[40] As White explains, legal formalism was a product of its time and was no longer viable once the "truths of early 20th century America were exposed as myths."[41] A leading indicator of this waning of legal formalism was the growing number of political actors willing to directly attack it, as evidenced by the Senate's response to Herbert Hoover's nominations of Charles Evans Hughes and John Parker to the Supreme Court in 1930. Although leading progressive senators such as Robert LaFollette and George Norris had used previous Supreme Court nominations as opportunities to rail against the jurisprudence of the Fuller, White, and Taft Courts, these efforts never resulted in more than a handful of senators voting against confirmation. In contrast, although Hughes was also confirmed after what was been described as "the most bitter debate over confirmation of a chief justice…in the history of the United States," the fact that 26 senators cast their votes against an otherwise impeccably qualified and scandal-free nominee was indicative of the extent to which legal formalism had become politically toxic.[42] This toxicity was evident in the rhetoric of Hughes' opponents, who warned that his confirmation would bolster the formalist majority on the Court and allow it to continue to declare needed economic regulatory legislation unconstitutional. Thus, Senator William Borah highlighted the "extreme views held by Mr. Hughes in defense of property," views that allowed "practically no restraint…upon the vast corporate interests" while Senator Carter Glass asserted that Hughes' record as a judge revealed a "perfect antipathy to the rights of the states."[43] Opponents of the nomination also attacked legal formalism's pretense of neutrality, with Senator Clarence Dill arguing that it was time to openly acknowledge that the members of the Court are "men like other men" who "write their economic views into decisions" and Senator Robert LaFollette, Jr. arguing that in light of this reality it was "imperative…to weigh the economic and social views of Mr. Hughes."[44]

Similarly, although the Senate's rejection of the Parker nomination later in the same year is largely remembered as a rejection of Parker's views on race, the nomination is also noteworthy for the extent to which Democrats and progressive Republicans once again "use[d] the confirmation process as an opportunity to attack the Court's doctrine."[45] The impetus for these attacks was provided by Parker's majority opinion in *United Mine Workers of America v. Red Jacket Consolidated Coal & Coke Company*, in which the 4th Circuit Court of Appeals upheld an injunction against a labor union's campaign to induce workers to break "yellow dog" employment contracts forbidding unionization. Although Parker's opinion merely followed precedent established by the Supreme Court, it provided another opportunity for senators to register their opposition to legal formalism.

Thus, opponents of the nomination cast Parker as but the latest in a long line of "injunction judges" who had constitutionalized their laissez faire economic views, with Senator Henry Ashurst denouncing the Court's liberty of contract jurisprudence as "precedent that...enslave[s] men who are unable to help themselves."[46] Parker's defeat also signaled the coming realignment of American politics. Although Republicans held 56 Senate seats while Democrats held only 41, the nomination was nonetheless rejected by a vote of 49 to 47. Despite the fact that 11 Southern Democrats voted in favor of Parker's confirmation, his defeat was ensured by the fact that 22 Republicans voted against him. These senators' decision to break with the majority of their caucus and with their president was illustrative of the deepening divide within a declining Republican regime between "Old Guard" and "agrarian insurgent" factions and of the fact that effective control of the Senate now rested with a coalition of Democrats and progressive Republicans.[47]

Conversely, the overwhelmingly positive response to Hoover's subsequent nomination of Benjamin Cardozo, who was confirmed in 1932 by a unanimous vote, was also indicative of the turning of public opinion against legal formalism. Not only was Cardozo's nomination received enthusiastically by the Senate, it was also received enthusiastically by the legal profession and by the public at large, with the New York Times noting that "seldom, if ever, in the history of the Court has an appointment been so universally commended."[48] This acclimation extended to the elite ranks of the legal academy, as Cardozo's nomination had come in response to lobbying on his behalf by a number of prominent academics, including the deans of the Harvard, Yale, and Columbia law schools.[49] This response was significant given Cardozo's background. In addition to his service as chief judge of the New York Court of Appeals, Cardozo had gained prominence as the author of *The Nature of the Judicial Process*, which critiques legal formalism and forthrightly discusses the role of considerations of public policy and subconscious attitudinal influences in judging.[50] Indeed, the debate that Cardozo's account of the judicial process precipitated has been identified by a number of legal historians as a critical moment portending the realist turn in legal thought.[51] Thus, the very fact of Cardozo's nomination and the response to it were indicative of a changing legal (and political) climate.

This new climate would contribute to significant changes to law school curricula. Leading the way in the effort to "apply sociological jurisprudence to legal education" was Columbia Law School, which in the early 1920s began to organize material in its courses along functional lines that crossed traditional conceptual boundaries between subjects.[52] This was coupled with an increased emphasis upon statutory material and upon sociological and economic data. These innovations had their immediate origins in the leadership of university president Nicholas Murray Butler, who publicly challenged the law school in his 1922 president's report, which declared that "legal education has fallen into the ruts" and should have its curriculum subjected to "searching criticism…as has been the case with letters and science."[53] Butler's call for reforming legal education by bringing it into accord with trends in the social sciences were consistent with efforts to change Columbia's law school from within by Herman Oliphant, who prior to his election as president of the Association of American Law Schools had spearheaded the transformation of the law school's curriculum. These efforts were complemented by the hiring of a number of new faculty members closely identified with the legal realist movement, such as William Douglas and Roswell Magill, who added to an existing cadre of prominent realists that included, in addition to Oliphant, Karl Llewellyn, Underhill Moore, and Hessel Yntema.

The realist curriculum that was developed at Columbia Law School would influence curricula at other elite law schools, particularly Yale Law School. This was in large part the result of several of the realists on Columbia Law School's faculty resigning and moving to Yale, which subsequently became the center of the legal realist movement, following a dispute with Butler in 1928 regarding the selection of the law school's new dean.[54] While Harvard Law School, the birthplace of the case method and the home of such prominent formalists as Joseph Beale and Samuel Williston, was widely viewed as a conservative and tradition-bound institution at the time, the composition of its faculty also took a realist turn in the 1920s. Although Kalman concludes that the brand of legal realism that swept Columbia and Yale "won no converts at Harvard," the law school did add a number of notable anti-formalists to its faculty.[55] Perhaps the most prominent of these were Felix Frankfurter, whose innovative functionalist approach to teaching administrative law drew criticism from Harvard Law School's traditionalists, and James Landis, whose groundbreaking statistical analyses of Supreme Court decision-making were a harbinger of empirical trends in legal scholarship while other faculty known for their more realist orientation who were hired during this period were Thomas Reed Powell, who aroused controversy at the law school by explaining Supreme Court doctrine to his students primarily in terms of the political values of the justices, and George Gardner, whose functionalist approach to studying contracts was instrumental in bridging traditional conceptual boundaries between contract and tort law.[56] Nonetheless, in comparison to other elite law schools Harvard Law School would continue to remain relatively traditional throughout the 1920s and 30s in terms of its curriculum, with fewer courses adopting a functional approach and fewer courses attempting to integrate law and the social sciences.[57]

RESISTANCE TO LEGAL REALISM

The capture by the legal realist movement of the elite law schools that play a disproportionate role in shaping legal thought contrasted sharply with the continued conservatism of most non-elite law schools. Given these law schools' greater emphasis on practical training and preparation for bar examinations, their administrators and faculty generally viewed legal realism as at best a distraction and at worst a serious threat to legal education. As Walter Kennedy of Fordham Law School warned, if the "rule of men" advocated by legal realists prevailed, there would be "no law to teach."[58] This aversion to the realist trend at non-elite law schools was shared by the nation's leading legal professional organization, the American Bar Association. In contrast to its contemporary image as a liberal organization, the image of the American Bar Association of the 1920s and 1930s was of a "rigidly conservative" organization and its leadership was quite vocal in its opposition to the New Deal and to legal realism.[59] Thus, just as American Bar Association President William Ransom would characterize the New Deal as a "blue print borrowed from old world dictatorship," James Rogers, the chairman of the American Bar Association's Committee on Legal Education, observed with dismay that legal realism threatened to profoundly alter legal education.[60]

The increasing prominence of legal realism in the legal academy during the 1920s also contributed to tension of a more general sort between practitioners and academics, with the leaders of the American

Bar Association engaging in regular denunciations of the faculty of elite law schools as "dangerous academic theorists" who were undermining the "safety and security of constitutional government."[61] This hostility toward legal realism was not merely a product of the conservative politics of the American Bar Association's leadership but also a product of these leaders' concerns regarding the place of the legal profession in a realist world. As legal realism's deconstruction of legal reasoning and the judicial process challenged the worth of the "theoretical knowledge on which the intellectual authority of the legal profession had traditionally been based," the American Bar Association's rhetorical campaign against legal realism represented in large part a defensive rearguard effort to preserve the status of the legal profession.[62]

The organized legal profession's resistance to the realist trend that was sweeping elite law schools also contained an important cultural component. As Shamir explains, legal realism, especially in light of the appointment of several prominent realists to powerful positions in the Roosevelt administration, was widely associated with the rise of a "new counter-elite of Jews, Catholics, and second generation immigrants."[63] The rise of this new counter-elite was accelerated by the New Deal, which offered opportunities in government service to lawyers not part of the corporate bar's traditional professional elite.[64] The negative reaction to legal realism among the leaders of the organized legal profession therefore also represented part of a broader backlash against this unprecedented exercise of power and influence by members of groups that had historically been excluded from the elite ranks of the legal profession. However, this acrimony between the organized bar and elite law schools was not unique to or solely a consequence of the bar's distaste for legal realism. As an institution long characterized by its resistance to change, the organized bar had consistently opposed almost every major innovation in legal education. Indeed, there had been considerable resistance within the organized bar in the late 19th and early 20th centuries to the law schools' introduction of the case method, with the American Bar Association criticizing it as "too technical" and as neglecting the "higher duties of…[the] profession and citizenship," and the Association of American Law Schools was formed in 1900 in direct response to the intractability of these differences regarding the direction of legal education.[65]

POLITICAL SUPPORT FOR LEGAL REALISM

Although the leaders of the organized bar continued to attack legal realism throughout the 1930s, the relationship between the legal realist movement and the leadership of the political branches of government would change significantly following the election of Franklin Roosevelt and the Democratic Party's capture of the presidency and both houses of Congress in 1932. Whereas the deposed Republican regime had, despite its significant progressive faction, generally been associated with legal formalism, the Democratic regime that emerged from the 1932 election would wholeheartedly embrace the realist trend in law. While the courts were not a prominent theme of Roosevelt's campaign, Roosevelt made a number of statements that signaled his agreement with realist critiques of the Supreme Court. For example, in a major campaign speech entitled "Destruction, Delay, Deceit, and Despair," Roosevelt pointedly included the Supreme Court among the branches of government controlled by the Republican Party that he held responsible for the crisis facing the nation.[66] Just as Roosevelt's implicit characterization of the Court as a political institution echoed the arguments of legal realists, the Republican response to Roosevelt's speech echoed the arguments of legal realism's critics, with Herbert Hoover accusing Roosevelt of "weaken[ing] respect" for the Court as an institution" and reducing it to an "instrument of party policy."[67] Roosevelt's efforts during the campaign to articulate an alternative constitutional vision also echoed the arguments of legal realists insofar as they spoke of the Constitution as a living document that should be interpreted in light of modern economic and social realities. This early embrace of legal realism's functionalist view of the law was evident in Roosevelt's 1932 speech before the Commonwealth Club, in which he declared that the Constitution must not be allowed to ossify and become a "barrier to progress" but rather should serve as the "broad highway through which alone true progress may be enjoyed."[68]

These relatively subtle calls for legal change during Roosevelt's campaign would be followed by a much more explicit embrace of many of the ideas associated with legal realism once Roosevelt took office. The most visible aspect of this embrace was the appointment of a number of academics identified with the legal realist movement to prominent posts in the administration. These included such notable figures in the movement as Jerome Frank, the author of the seminal realist tract *Law and the Modern Mind*, William Douglas, whose functional approach to the law of business associations was an early exemplar of realist methodology, and Thurman Arnold, whose empirical studies of courts and judicial behavior epitomized the fusion of jurisprudence and social science that legal realism would become known for. They also included Edward Corwin, the former president of the American Political Science Association and one of the most prominent realists among political scientists studying judicial behavior. Most importantly, the legal ideology that these realists brought to their posts would play a key role in shaping the Roosevelt administration's legal agenda. This was evident at an early stage when Frank, who had been appointed general counsel of the Agricultural Adjustment Administration, was enlisted in 1934 to write the amicus brief that the administration submitted to the Supreme Court in the case of *Nebbia v. New York*. Affirming the constitutionality of the state of New York's regulation of milk prices, this decision represented a major step in the Court's abandonment of the doctrine of economic substantive due process. The influence of legal realism in the Roosevelt administration was also evident in the leading role that Corwin, in his capacity as a special assistant and consultant to Attorney General Homer Cummings, played in promoting Roosevelt's court-packing plan to Congress.[69]

These prominent appointments of legal realists were merely indicative of the deeper ties forged between the Roosevelt administration and the elite law schools at which legal realism flourished. These ties were personified by Felix Frankfurter, widely recognized as the "legal manager of the New Deal," who used the professional networks he developed as a faculty member at Harvard Law School to supply the administration with the dependably liberal lawyers needed to implement its legal agenda.[70] Imbued with the tenets of legal realism, these recent graduates of elite law schools played an indispensable role in staffing the myriad of new administrative agencies created as part of the New Deal.[71] Indeed, the role of academics identified with the legal realist movement in the Roosevelt administration would become a source of political controversy, with the administration's critics frequently citing these academics' controversial scholarly writings as evidence of the administration's radicalism.[72]

As suggestive as these associations were, the relationship between the Roosevelt administration's legal agenda and legal realism would not truly come to the fore until the administration's public confrontation with the Supreme Court. As his implicit criticism of the Court during his 1932 campaign indicated, Roosevelt was wary of the Court even early in his presidency and was slow to bring cases involving constitutional challenges to New Deal legislation before the Court.[73] Indeed, Roosevelt had privately explored ways of restricting or abolishing the Court's power of judicial review and "packing" lower federal courts with his advisors as early as 1933.[74] This wariness would be vindicated by the Court delivering several decisions in 1935 that declared major pieces of New Deal legislation unconstitutional. Confronted with a Court whose formalistic interpretation of the Constitution obstructed much of its legislative agenda, the Roosevelt administration responded by advancing arguments first developed by legal realists regarding the need for jurisprudence to show more appreciation for the factual context of cases than for abstract principles. For example, Attorney General Homer Cummings's condemnation of the Court's jurisprudence in his 1935 speech before the American Bar Association was premised upon his assertion that the Court "does not operate in a legalistic vacuum" but rather "is part and parcel of an organic process of government."[75] Roosevelt's own rhetoric also drew upon the language of legal realism, lamenting the fact that the Court had consigned the nation to an antiquated "horse and buggy definition of interstate commerce," analogizing the Court's approach to constitutional interpretation to "old glasses fitted…for the needs of another generation," and speaking of the need for a new style of jurisprudence informed by "modern facts and circumstances."[76]

Rhetoric aside, Roosevelt's legislative response to the Court's rejection of the New Deal, the Judicial Procedures Reform Bill of 1937's court-packing plan, was also indicative of the influence of legal realism. The fact that the Roosevelt administration responded to the invalidation of the National Recovery Act and other New Deal initiatives by attempting to "pack" the Court rather than by pursuing a constitutional amendment reflected not only political expediency but also a realist belief in constitutional uncertainty and flexibility, Indeed, prominent realists such as Thurman Arnold and John Dickinson were among the strongest opponents of constitutionalizing the New Deal by amending the Constitution, critiquing such a course of action as potentially counterproductive and arguing in favor of treating the Constitution as a living document that could be interpreted in accordance with contemporary realities as is.[77]

UNDERSTANDING THE RELATIONSHIP BETWEEN THE NEW DEAL REGIME AND THE RISE OF THE LEGAL REALIST MOVEMENT

Roosevelt's place in history as a reconstructive president who attempted to reconstruct the constitutional order by promoting legal realism presents a number of parallels to the efforts of Ronald Reagan to reconstruct the constitutional order by promoting originalism. In order to measure the timing and magnitude of the realist turn in legal thought and assess the contribution of Roosevelt's support, an analysis was conducted of the number of realist publications and the number of publications critiquing legal realism appearing in the three most influential law reviews over a ten-year period bracketing Roosevelt's assumption of the presidency and the beginnings of his efforts to promote constitutional change in 1933.

Given the considerable diversity in terms of outlook and emphasis among the scholars that have been counted as legal realists and their prominent internecine conflicts, legal realism was defined broadly. Specifically, realist publications were defined as publications that espouse an anti-formalist and functional approach to the law that emphasizes the need for the law to adapt to the realities of contemporary society and that recognizes the role of public policy considerations and attitudinal influences in the judicial process. This coding protocol counted as realist publications that critique existing legal doctrine for being rooted in artificial and/or antiquated concepts and that embrace a more context-sensitive and dynamic approach. For example, these included Arnold's article on the restatement of the law of trusts, which asserts that "no closed philosophical system of the law of trusts is possible" and that the "ancient" concepts underlying the law of trusts must be evaluated "in light of [their] utility in solving modern problems," and Cohen's more emphatic dismissal of such concepts as "transcendental nonsense."[78] Most importantly, they also included critiques of formalist approaches to constitutional interpretation and calls for interpreting the Constitution as a living document, such as Llewellyn's characterization of contemporary constitutional doctrine as an "outworn, performance-baffling framework" that "once had some point and value" but has "ceased to serve" and Lerner's characterization of the Constitution as a "broad pathway of government rather than a fixed and narrow code of law."[79]

Realist publications also included the numerous critical reviews of casebooks and treatises that to realists embodied a formalistic approach to legal education. Typical of these is Yntema's review of Beale's casebook on the conflict of laws, which asserts that Beale's search for an "eternal general principle" is based upon "an illusion," that such a principle would in any event be "so general as to be of little practical use in controlling the activities of courts and lawyers" and that "the purpose of legal education…is not…to establish so-called fundamental principles of law" but rather to "awaken…social responsiveness."[80] Conversely, realist publications also included numerous positive reviews of casebooks and treatises that employ the functional approach favored by realists, such as, for example, Swaine's review of a casebook on the law of corporations co-authored by William Douglas, in which he praises Douglas and his co-author for "spending more time analyzing practical problems and less time elaborating philosophical abstractions."[81] Finally, as perhaps the most significant insight of legal realism was its observation that abstract principles do not decide concrete cases, realist publications also included publications that attempt to a provide a more realistic account of the judicial process. Such accounts include, for example, Dickinson's account of the development of the common law, which attacks the "dogma that the courts do not and cannot make law" and argues that "unwritten law is the product of legislative discretion exercised by the courts."[82]

Publications coded as counter-realist were publications that directly critique legal realism, whether by critiquing legal realism on empirical grounds by arguing that it understates the extent to which rules and principles cabin judicial behavior or by critiquing legal realism on normative grounds by arguing that its instrumentalism is a threat to the rule of law. For example, among the most prominent critiques focusing upon legal realism's empirical shortcomings is Adler's article "Legal Certainty," which takes realists to task for their failure to appreciate how judicial discretion "operate[s] within the range of possible alternatives defined by an exhaustive analysis of the plurality of legal doctrines."[83] Conversely, among the most prominent normative critiques of legal realism is Pound's article "The Future of Law," which argues that the inevitable endpoint of legal realism's skepticism of legal concepts would be nothing less than a "society operating without law."[84]

The three law reviews selected for analysis were those that have historically combined both the greatest institutional prestige and the greatest citation impact. These included: Columbia Law Review, Harvard Law Review, and Yale Law Journal. These three publications also represent a particularly appropriate sample insofar as they each differ in the extent to which the faculties and administrations of their respective law schools embraced legal realism. While Columbia Law School was the early center of the nascent legal realist movement, it gradually turned away from legal realism beginning in the late 1920s as many of the scholars most strongly identified with legal realism relocated to Yale Law School, which subsequently assumed the mantle of realism. Conversely, Harvard Law School was generally perceived as the "center of resistance to all attempts to make legal education more 'realistic.'"[85] A total of 3,908 articles, book reviews, comments, and notes were published in these law reviews during the time period analyzed. A total of 363 of these publications were coded as realist. The annual number of realist publications is expressed as a percentage of the total number of articles, book reviews, comments, and notes appearing each year in these law reviews.

It was anticipated that the number of realist publications would begin to increase in the early 1930s on the heels of the anti-formalist political backlash associated with the Hughes and Parker nominations, a backlash that reflected popular disenchantment with the strictures placed by legal formalism upon the ability of the government to respond to the Great Depression. It was also anticipated that this increase in the amount of realist scholarship would be modest relative to the more significant increase that was expected to follow the launch of the New Deal in 1933 and the Roosevelt administration's embrace of legal realism. Another expectation was that this would set the stage for a continuous increase in the amount of realist scholarship over the course of the remainder of the 1930s as the New Deal regime consolidated and that this continuous increase would be punctuated by periodic surges in realist scholarship associated with events such as the Supreme Court's invalidation of several major pieces of New Deal legislation on "Black Monday" in 1935 and the 1937 debate on the Roosevelt administration's court-packing plan. Conversely, it was anticipated that the Roosevelt administration's embrace of legal realism would spur counter-mobilization by legal formalists that would be reflected in a significant increase in the amount of scholarship critiquing legal realism but that the number of such critiques would subsequently decline as legal formalism increasingly fell into popular and political disfavor over the course of the 1930s.

The results are consistent with some of these expectations and inconsistent with others. In particular, the results indicate that the anticipated change in the climate of the legal marketplace occurred in the early 1930s. This is reflected in the fact that the proportion of realist publications appearing in elite law reviews nearly doubled between 1929 and 1931. Moreover, the data indicate that this increase represented a general realist turn in the legal marketplace of ideas that was not limited to law reviews affiliated with law schools whose faculties and administrations embraced legal realism, as the percentage of publications appearing in the Harvard Law Review between 1928 and 1938 that were coded as realist (seven percent) was comparable to the percentages of publications appearing during the same period in the Columbia Law Review and Yale Law Journal that were coded as realist (10 and 11%, respectively). However, whereas the upsurge in originalist scholarship that occurred in the latter half of the 1980s is clearly attributable to the efforts of the Reagan administration to promote originalism, the relationship between the upsurge in realist scholarship that occurred in the 1930s and the Roosevelt administration's attacks on legal formalism is more tenuous. On the one hand, distinct spikes in realist scholarship followed the introduction of the New Deal in 1933, the Roosevelt administration's rhetorical attacks on the Supreme Court in 1935 following its spate of decisions declaring New Deal legislation unconstitutional, and the introduction of the administration's court-packing plan in 1937. Moreover, the impact of these external shocks on the legal marketplace of ideas would likely have been even greater if not for the recruitment of many of the most productive realist scholars into government service. Indeed, nearly a fifth (17%) of the realist publications appearing in elite law reviews prior to the New Deal were authored by scholars who would subsequently leave the academy for positions in the Roosevelt administration. These scholars included Thurman Arnold, William Douglas, Jerome Frank, Felix Frankfurter, James Landis, Roswell Magill, and Herman Oliphant.

However, on the other hand, these spikes in realist scholarship clearly built upon a foundation that had been laid prior to the Roosevelt administration (see Figure 3.1). In fact, the years that saw the largest upsurges in realist scholarship were 1930, the year in which such seminal realist tracts as Jerome Frank's *Law and the Modern Mind* and Karl Llewellyn's *The Bramble Bush* were published, and 1931, the year of Llewellyn and Roscoe Pound's famous exchange on legal realism in the pages of the Harvard Law Review. This realist breakthrough followed closely on the heels of the acrimonious Senate debates on the Hughes and Parker nominations, which saw legal formalism come under its most sustained and vociferous political attacks to date.

Figure 3.1: Legal Realist Publications Appearing in the 3 most Influential Law Reviews, 1928-38

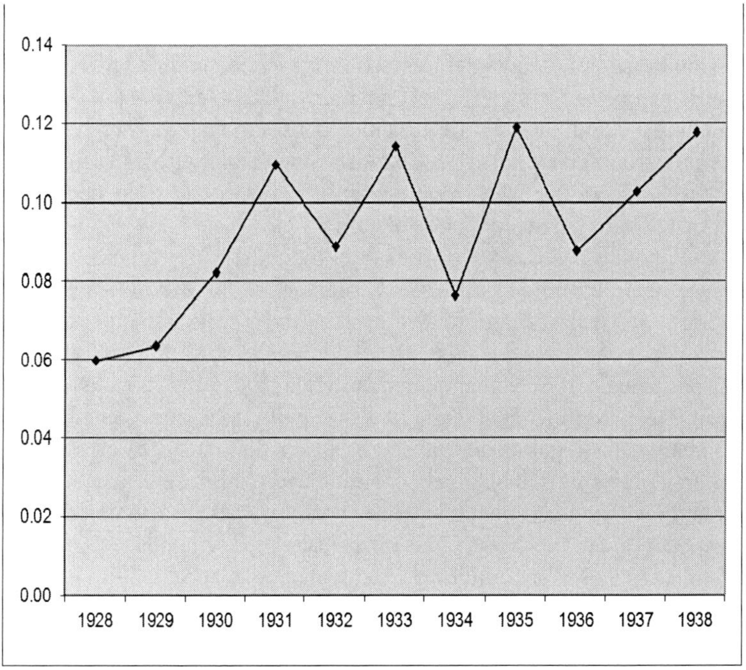

Moreover, this pattern persists even when the analysis is limited to realist publications that discuss constitutional issues and/or constitutional interpretation. Because the Roosevelt administration's efforts to promote legal change largely consisted of efforts to promote the idea of a living Constitution, they might therefore be expected to have had a more significant effect upon the amount of realist scholarship discussing constitutional issues and/or interpretation than upon the amount of realist scholarship discussing common law and statutory interpretation. Thus, a second analysis was conducted that was limited to these publications. A total of 545 of the articles, book reviews, comments, and notes published in the three law reviews between 1928 and 1938 discussed constitutional issues and/or interpretation, of which a total of 119 were coded as realist. The temporal distribution of these publications indicates that the growth of constitutional realism followed a pattern similar to that of the growth of legal realism generally. In particular, as was the case with the proportion of realist publications appearing in elite law reviews generally, the proportion of realist publications discussing constitutional issues and/or interpretation appearing in elite law reviews (as a percentage of the total number of articles, book reviews, comments, and notes discussing constitutional issues and/or interpretation appearing in elite law reviews) experienced its greatest growth prior to the New Deal, peaking in 1933 and then declining somewhat before plateauing (see Figure 3.2).

Thus, the Roosevelt administration's efforts to promote legal change are best understood as a continuation of the anti-formalist critiques that had been articulated by prominent progressive politicians for over two decades and that had given rise to sociological jurisprudence, critiques that gained particular traction as a result of the Great Depression. That legal realism built upon the considerable momentum for legal change in the academy that had been created by the proponents of sociological jurisprudence is also evidenced by the extent to which it dominated legal discourse and marginalized opposing perspectives on the law. This marginalization is indicated by the volume of scholarship critiquing legal realism that appeared in elite law reviews during the time period examined. The scarcity of such publications is suggestive of the depth of legal realism's entrenchment in the elite ranks of the legal academy. Unlike previous and subsequent realignments of the political system, the New Deal realignment did not see the pages of the law reviews become a major front in the unfolding ideological conflict. Whereas the Reagan administration's efforts to promote originalism provoked vigorous counter-mobilization by legal liberals that was reflected in the publication of a wave of attacks on originalism in the wake of Edwin Meese's speech to the American Bar

Association and the Bork nomination, legal realism's transformation of legal discourse went largely unchallenged in the legal academy's most prestigious publications.

Figure 3.2: Legal Realist Publications Discussing Constitutional Issues/Interpretation Appearing in the 3 most Influential Law Reviews, 1928-38

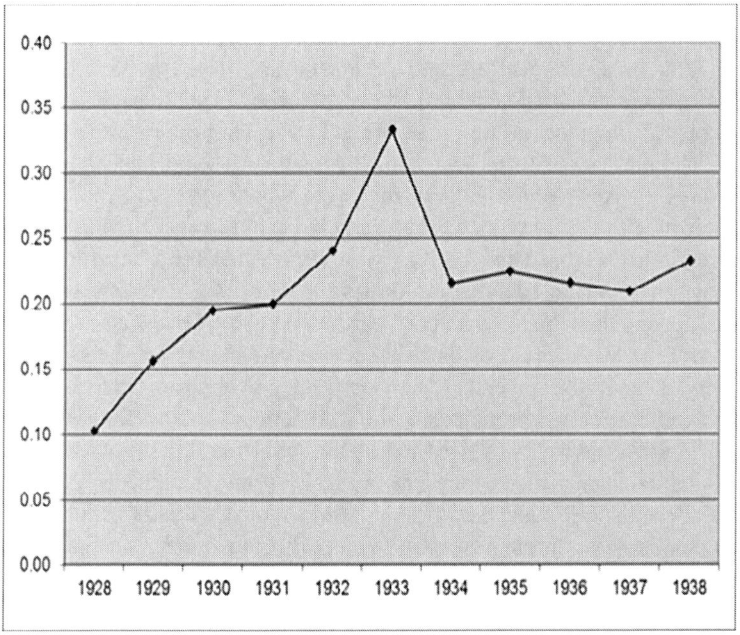

Indeed, only 13 critical publications appeared in these law reviews between 1928 and 1938, many of which were written by scholars who were generally sympathetic toward legal realism but who took issue with the more extreme assertions of some of its proponents. For example, three of these critical publications are the work of Roscoe Pound, whose call for a sociological jurisprudence had given voice to progressive opposition to legal formalism but who later became a critic of "radical neo-realism" for "deny[ing] that there are rules or principles or conceptions or doctrines at all."[86] Similarly, while Kantorowicz praises the "admirable achievements of the realists," he chides realists for ignoring the "invisible certainty of the law in the normal cases" while being "obsessed by the obvious uncertainty of the law in the few contested cases."[87] The nine qualified critiques of this variety significantly outnumbered the four more unequivocal critiques by scholars associated with legal formalism, such as Beale, Laughlin, Guthrie, and Sandomire's dismissal of legal realists as "our dogmatic friends who amuse themselves and others with…sterile metaphysical gymnastic[s]" and of legal realism as the "ponderous exactitude of the behaviorists."[88]

The data are also significant insofar as they cast doubt upon Tamanaha's recent assessment of the place of legal realism in legal history. Tamanaha argues that the legal realist movement did not fundamentally transform legal thought insofar as legal realists merely "expressed views about judging that were typical of their generation," albeit in a "rebellious tone" that garnered attention.[89] Similar views have been expressed by Rabban, who argues that the transition from legal formalism to sociological jurisprudence to legal realism was far less abrupt than historians have portrayed it, by Dworkin, who has referred to the success of the legal realist movement in changing the terms of legal discourse as a "famous victory over straw persons," and by Kalman, who pronounces the movement an intellectual and pedagogical failure.[90] While there is no doubt that the arguments and insights of legal realists were not original but rather built upon earlier anti-formalist critiques, the surge in anti-formalist scholarship indicates that it was not until the rise of the legal realist movement and change in the political environment that these critiques gained broader acceptance in the elite ranks of the legal academy.

This change in the climate of the legal marketplace of ideas is also reflected in the change in the tone of anti-formalist critiques, a change that illustrates the subtle differences between sociological jurisprudence and legal realism. The proponents of sociological jurisprudence were, despite their iconoclasm, products of their time insofar as they retained considerable faith in the ability of the judicial process to produce consistent and predictable results. For example, although Cardozo's declaration in *The Nature of the Judicial Process* that law "is not found, but made" was a source of controversy, his conception of the judicial process was relatively mechanical and he took care to emphasize the "narrow range of choice" available to judges.[91] Thus, as Horwitz explains, while Cardozo analogized the judge to a pharmacist whose role it was to "slip a few more ingredients of 'humanness' into the remedy," he and other proponents of sociological jurisprudence did not believe that it was the role of the judge to "reconsider the fundamental structure."[92] In contrast, legal realists were more skeptical of the ability of judges to separate law and politics, placing greater emphasis upon the inherent contradictions of all legal concepts and expressing a more pessimistic attitude toward law as an instrument of reform.

Examining reviews of *The Nature of the Judicial Process*, which was the most widely read and reviewed work by any of the scholars associated with sociological jurisprudence, and of *Law and the Modern Mind* and *The Bramble Bush*, which were the first works to use the term "legal realism" and which have been credited with "proclaim[ing] the arrival of a new movement in legal thought," this change in the climate of the legal marketplace of ideas is evident.[93] While the response to *The Nature of the Judicial Process* was largely positive given Cardozo's esteemed place in the legal profession, this response was also somewhat apprehensive even of Cardozo's relatively nuanced brand of realism. For example, Hand, although complimentary of Cardozo's forthrightness in "frankly own[ing] the way in which he works," recognizes the extent to which Cardozo's views challenge conceptions of the judicial process that were prevalent at the time, noting that "there is a scandal in so much subjectivity" and that "there are excellent people who cannot help but feeling that the voice of this book is…the voice of heresy."[94] This despite Cardozo's assurance that there is "nothing revolutionary or even novel" about his conception of the judicial process.[95] Similarly, while Burch praises Cardozo for drawing attention to the role of public policy considerations and subconscious attitudinal influences in the judicial process, he criticizes Cardozo for overstating the malleability of the law and for providing an "[in]adequate conception of the limitations on the judge's function as formulator of law."[96]

While the response to the restrained realism of *The Nature of the Judicial Process* is indicative of the intellectual climate faced by the proponents of sociological jurisprudence, the response to the uncompromising realism of *Law and the Modern Mind* and *The Bramble Bush* is indicative of the changes in the intellectual climate that occurred over the course of the intervening decade. Ascribing the "absurdly unrealistic notion that law is…certain and…predictable" to a "childish desire to recapture a father-controlled world," *Law and the*

Modern Mind was written in a bold and provocative style that was often derided as "shocking and intemperate" and in "bad taste."[97] Yet despite the misgivings most reviewers expressed about its tone, *Law and the Modern Mind* was generally received as an important work exposing misconceptions regarding the nature of the judicial process. This assessment was not limited to confirmed realists such as Llewellyn, who hails *Law and the Modern Mind* as "unique in attempting exploration of emotional drives and genetic psychology for their contribution to our understanding of the ways of the law."[98] Thus, although Cox dismisses Frank's efforts to apply insights from child psychology to the study of judicial behavior as "a well-meaning kind of nonsense," he lauds the timeliness of *Law and the Modern Mind*'s explication of the uncertainty and flexibility of the law, noting that "in a society undergoing as much change as ours there is less guidance to be obtained from the past."[99] Even Rottschaefer's more critical review, which concludes that *Law and the Modern Mind* "contains few new ideas," accepts the substance of Frank's critique of legal formalism, acknowledging its success in "indicating the dangers of legal fundamentalism."[100] The response to *The Bramble Bush* followed a similar pattern, with Llewellyn's style, which Horwitz characterizes as "ponderous rendition," giving rise to some critical commentary but his call for a more realistic conception of the law and the judicial process largely accepted.[101] Thus, Frank dubs it a "worthy successor…to Holmes's 'The Path of the Law'" while Corbin commends Llewellyn for exposing the "grotesque reasoning" of legal formalists and pronounces *The Bramble Bush* "the best introductory lectures the reviewer has seen."[102] This lack of formalist critiques indicates that while the realists' rebellious tone may have aroused some controversy, their basic approach to the law had become relatively uncontroversial by the early 1930s.

Legal realism's ascendancy in the legal profession is also reflected in the relative ease with which Franklin Roosevelt was able to use Supreme Court appointments to remake the Court. Whereas the New Right regime faced a judicial supply-side problem that initially prevented it from translating control of the judicial appointment process into a more conservative jurisprudence, the New Deal regime faced fewer problems in this regard. Unlike the Burger Court, whose jurisprudence frequently disappointed conservatives despite its Republican majority, the jurisprudence of the Stone and Vinson Courts was generally agreeable to most elements of the New Deal coalition. This can be attributed not only to the dominance of realist conceptions of the law in the legal profession but also to the political dominance of the New Deal regime, particularly the fact that every Supreme Court justice nominated by a Democratic president during the New Deal regime faced confirmation in a Senate with a large Democratic majority. Thus, while Republican presidents saw Democratic-controlled Senates reject their Supreme Court nominees on several occasions during the New Right regime, Democratic presidents faced no such problems during the New Deal regime as every nominee put forth by a Democratic president during this period was confirmed and none had more than 16 votes cast against them. The only setback in shaping the Court that was suffered by a Democratic president during this period was Lyndon Johnson's failed attempt to elevate Justice Abe Fortas to the chief justiceship, which was successfully filibustered by a coalition of Republicans and Southern Democrats and ultimately withdrawn. Occurring against the backdrop of the disintegration of the New Deal regime amidst the turmoil of 1968, this setback signaled the coming realignment of American politics.

The Democratic Party's lock on Congress during the New Deal regime thus gave Democratic presidents unparalleled latitude to create a Supreme Court that reflected their constitutional vision. Thus, for both Franklin Roosevelt and Harry Truman there was one overriding consideration in selecting Supreme Court nominees: validating the New Deal by selecting nominees who took an expansive view of federal regulatory authority under the Constitution and in this respect they invariably "got what [they] wanted."[103] Once the conservative "four horsemen" who had so frustrated Roosevelt retired and were replaced by Roosevelt's own appointees, the Court would display a remarkable level of consensus in cases involving issues relating to the scope of federal power. Thus, revolutionary decisions such as *United States v. Darby* and *Wickard v. Filburn*, which saw the Court adopt a posture of total deference to congressional assertions of regulatory authority under the Interstate Commerce Clause, were delivered with relatively little fanfare and by unanimous decision. Indeed, after the Court signaled the end of the Lochner era with its 1937 decision in *West Coast Hotel Company v. Parrish*, this principle of New Deal constitutionalism would become so entrenched that it would not be until the Court's decision in *United States v. Lopez*, nearly 60 years later, that the Court would again declare an act of Congress unconstitutional on grounds that it was beyond the scope of the regulatory authority conferred by the Interstate Commerce Clause.

Roosevelt's appointees to the Court also shared a commitment to civil rights that distinguished them from the jurists they replaced. Although the political clout wielded by Southern Democrats in the New Deal coalition initially prevented legislative action on civil rights, Roosevelt was able to use the powers of the presidency to attack segregation and racial discrimination in the South, establishing the Department of Justice's Civil Rights Division and appointing judges more sympathetic to civil rights claims.[104] This led the Roosevelt Court to take an unprecedentedly active role in the protection of civil rights, delivering a number of decisions that foreshadowed *Brown v. Board of Education* by limiting the doctrine of "separate but equal" in education, such as *Gaines v. Canada*, *McLaurin v. Oklahoma State Regents*, and *Sweatt v. Painter*, and a number of decisions that alleviated the political disenfranchisement of African Americans in the South, such as *Smith v. Allwright*, which abolished the "white primary."

However, despite its unanimity in certain areas of the law, the Court was by no means an ideologically monolithic institution during this period. Just as there were significant jurisprudential cleavages among the Republicans appointed to the Court during the New Right regime, the Democrats appointed to the Court during the New Deal regime were similarly divided. Moreover, just as would later be the case with the New Right regime, generational replacement on the Court over the course of the life cycle of the regime would lead to significant ideological change. Both of these dynamics were illustrated by calculating measures of the ideology of each justice appointed during the New Deal regime using Martin and Quinn's estimations of each justice's ideal point in ideological space for each term (see Table 3.2). While Hugo Black, William Douglas, Frank Murphy, and Wiley Rutledge were early exemplars of the activist liberal constitutionalism that the Warren Court would later popularize, the majority of the justices appointed by Roosevelt and Truman were centrists and conservatives who embodied a very different legal ideology.

Table 3.2: Supreme Court Appointments during the New Deal Regime

Name	*Appointed*	*President*	*Ideology*	*Born*	*Admitted to Bar*
Hugo Black	1937	F. Roosevelt	−1.76	1886	1906
Stanley Reed	1938	F. Roosevelt	0.36	1884	1910
Felix Frankfurter	1939	F. Roosevelt	0.53	1882	1906
William Douglas	1939	F. Roosevelt	−4.15	1898	1925
Frank Murphy	1940	F. Roosevelt	−1.59	1890	1914
James Byrnes	1941	F. Roosevelt	−0.19	1882	1903
Robert Jackson	1941	F. Roosevelt	0.73	1892	1913
Wiley Rutledge	1943	F. Roosevelt	−1.40	1894	1922
Harold Burton	1945	Truman	1.02	1888	1912
Fred Vinson	1946	Truman	1.00	1890	1911
Tom Clark	1949	Truman	0.48	1899	1922
Sherman Minton	1949	Truman	1.10	1890	1916
Earl Warren	1953	Eisenhower	−1.18	1891	1914
John Harlan	1955	Eisenhower	1.64	1899	1925
William Brennan	1956	Eisenhower	−1.94	1906	1931
Charles Whittaker	1957	Eisenhower	1.26	1901	1924
Potter Stewart	1958	Eisenhower	0.56	1915	1941
Byron White	1962	Kennedy	0.44	1917	1946
Arthur Goldberg	1962	Kennedy	−0.79	1908	1930
Abe Fortas	1965	Johnson	−1.20	1910	1933
Thurgood Marshall	1967	Johnson	−2.83	1908	1933

In particular, these ideological differences reflected a deep divide on the Court between proponents of judicial restraint, led by Felix Frankfurter and Robert Jackson, and proponents of judicial activism, led by Hugo Black and William Douglas.[105] While both groups of justices could agree on a posture of deference and restraint in cases involving economic regulation, they differed on whether this deferential approach should be applied across the board. For the Court's centrists and conservatives, "the core principle of American constitutional democracy was majoritarianism and the chief danger was judicial tyranny."[106] Thus, their deference in cases involving economic regulation was reflective of a broader commitment to judicial restraint, even in cases involving denials of constitutional rights and liberties, cases in which they were willing to set aside their own political values. Thus, despite Frankfurter's background as a co-founder of the American Civil Liberties Union, he was consistently the member of the Court least willing to vindicate individual rights claims, writing the majority opinion in *Minersville School District v. Gobitis*, in which the Court affirmed the constitutionality of laws requiring students to salute the American flag, and writing a sharply worded concurring opinion in *Dennis v. United* States, in which the Court rejected the 1st Amendment claims of Communist Party leaders convicted of engaging in subversive speech. As Frankfurter declared in his majority opinion in *Colegrove v. Green*, these justices believed that "[c]ourts ought not to enter [the] political thicket" except in extraordinary cases because to do so would undermine their institutional authority and legitimacy.[107] This was a worldview shaped by the negative example of the Lochner Court, which was in its most activist phase as these justices began their legal careers. It was also shaped by the positive examples of Justice Oliver Wendell Holmes and Justice Louis Brandeis, who were heroes to a generation of progressive lawyers for their calls for judges to "refrain from allowing their...prejudices to overrule the proper policymaking role of elected officials."[108]

However, for the Court's smaller bloc of liberals, deference in cases involving economic regulation merely reflected their views regarding the constitutional balance between federal and state power and the desirability of such regulation. Thus, they were quite willing to use judicial power to vindicate non-economic constitutional rights and liberties, even when this would place the Court in conflict with the elected branches of government. This approach was exemplified by

Chief Justice Harlan Stone's opinion in *United States v. Carolene Products Company*, which attempted to articulate a principled rationale for this partial embrace of judicial activism by drawing a distinction between economic rights and liberties and "preferred freedoms or fundamental rights that are essential to the democratic process or to individual human dignity."[109] The issue that most frequently brought the conflict between these competing conceptions of the judicial role to the surface was the question of the incorporation of the Bill of Rights against state governments through the 14th Amendment's Due Process Clause. While Hugo Black, Frank Murphy, and Wiley Rutledge were the leading advocates of total incorporation, an approach that would have invalidated a broad range of criminal procedure laws at the state level, Felix Frankfurter and Robert Jackson were the leading advocates of a more restrained approach that would only require the states to incorporate those rights that were, in the words of Benjamin Cardozo's majority opinion in *Palko v. Connecticut*, "implicit in the concept of ordered liberty."[110]

These differences did not go unnoticed by Franklin Roosevelt and Harry Truman. The fact that all four of the justices appointed by Truman joined the Court's bloc of centrists and conservatives and thereby prevented the Court from assuming a more active role in enforcing constitutional rights and liberties led Truman to be particularly vocal in expressing his disappointment. Truman publicly lamented that "packing the Supreme Court simply can't be done…I've tried and it won't work…[w]henever you put a man on the Supreme Court he ceases to be your friend."[111] He also referred to his appointment of Tom Clark as the "biggest mistake" of his presidency on several occasions.[112] Thus, although they succeeded in realizing their primary objective of validating the New Deal, Roosevelt and Truman's success in using Supreme Court nominations to advance a consistently liberal constitutional vision was otherwise somewhat uneven.

This dynamic would begin to change with the rise of a new generation of lawyers that had received its legal training during legal realism's rise to prominence in the 1920s and 30s, a generation of lawyers that had been inculcated with a less rigid conception of the distinction between law and politics. As Kalman notes, many realists believed that "having exposed judges for what they were, they could engage in judicial activism with a clear conscience when they themselves became judges."[113] This attitude was exemplified in the jurisprudence of William Douglas, who was both a disciple of the legal realist movement, having studied at Columbia Law School during the movement's nascent years in the early 1920s, and one of its leading lights, subsequently joining Columbia's faculty and gaining renown as a proponent of functionalism. Once Douglas joined the Supreme Court, the contrast between his jurisprudence and that of the other prominent realist scholar on the Court, Felix Frankfurter, demonstrated that just as legal realism could serve as the foundation for a philosophy of judicial restraint, it could also serve as the foundation for a philosophy of judicial activism. While the lesson that Frankfurter drew from realism's insight of the political nature of the judicial process was that judges should avoid substituting their political judgments for those of elected officials whenever possible, the lesson that Douglas drew from this insight was that judges should simply be more forthright in articulating the bases for their decisions. Thus, Douglas's jurisprudence gained attention for the unprecedented extent to which it put this principle into action, eschewing reliance upon conventional sources of legal authority such as text, history, and precedent, which many realists had dismissed as mere pretenses for decisions reached on other grounds, in favor of reliance upon sociological analysis.[114]

This freewheeling approach initially set Douglas apart from his fellow justices. However, it would become much less of an anomaly as more members of Douglas's generation joined the Court and would set the tone for the Warren Court's subsequent "adventures in constitutional law-making."[115] This reflected the fact that for the most part the justices who received their legal training during the heyday of legal realism would embody the realism of Douglas rather than the realism of Frankfurter. Indeed, a number of these justices' realism had been forged in the centers of the legal realist movement during the movement's rise in the late 1920s and early 1930s. These included William Brennan, who studied at Harvard Law School under such prominent realists as James Landis, Thomas Reed Powell, and George Gardner and Abe Fortas, who studied at Yale Law School under such prominent realists as Thurman Arnold and William Douglas. This generational replacement corresponded to change in the dynamics of the judicial supply-side problem. While Democrats were occasionally disappointed with the conservatism of some of Franklin Roosevelt and Harry Truman's Supreme Court appointees, Republicans were even more disappointed with the liberalism of some of Dwight Eisenhower's Supreme Court appointees.

Not only did Eisenhower appoint Earl Warren, a decision he later described as the "biggest damned fool mistake I ever made," on the basis of his erroneous belief that Warren would be a conservative force for judicial restraint, he also appointed William Brennan, who would quickly emerge as the intellectual leader of the Court's liberal bloc, on the basis of erroneous assurances by his advisors regarding Brennan's supposedly conservative judicial philosophy.[116] In contrast to Eisenhower's difficulties in identifying prospective Supreme Court nominees who shared his constitutional values, John F. Kennedy and Lyndon Johnson had fewer problems in this regard. Although Byron White would establish a centrist record on the Court and broke with the Court's liberal bloc in a few important cases such as *Miranda v. Arizona* and *Roe v. Wade*, Arthur Goldberg, Abe Fortas, and Thurgood Marshall would establish strongly liberal records that were typical of their generation of lawyers.

CONCLUSIONS

The dynamics underlying the relationship between the rise of the legal realist movement and the Roosevelt administration's efforts to promote legal change differ in important respects from the dynamics underlying the relationship between the rise of the conservative legal movement and the Reagan administration's efforts to promote legal change. The Reagan administration's campaign for a jurisprudence of original intention was a necessary precursor to the broader acceptance of originalism given the overwhelmingly liberal character of the elite ranks of the legal academy and the lack of previous political support for originalism. This campaign was also critical to the legitimation of originalism given the relative weakness of the New Right regime, particularly in congressional elections, and its consequent inability to fully reconstruct the political order. This compelled the executive branch to assume more of a vanguard role in promoting originalism. In contrast, the Roosevelt administration's embrace of legal realism was less critical to realism's rise insofar as it came in the wake of a long line of attacks on legal formalism by progressives in both major political parties and of the emergence of sociological jurisprudence as a major strain of legal thought. This embrace of legal realism was also relatively less important due to the depth of the political realignment that was taking place at the time, a realignment that reduced the New Deal regime's conservative opponents to a powerless and insignificant minority. Taking advantage of the space created in the legal marketplace of ideas for anti-formalist critiques by the proponents of sociological jurisprudence, legal realists built upon their insights to develop an even more radical critique of classical legal thought, one that would come to dominate legal discourse. This was facilitated not only by the efforts of individuals in positions of authority in elite law schools such as Herman Oliphant and Nicholas Murray Butler but also by broader social, academic, and political trends. Not only had many of the assumptions underlying legal formalism been discredited by the Great Depression and by the evolution of the American legal system, formalism was also increasingly out of sync with trends in the social sciences toward functionalism and behaviorism. These developments, particularly the widely perceived need for economic regulatory legislation created by the Great Depression, led to an unprecedented escalation of political attacks on legal formalism, attacks that were epitomized by the unexpectedly hostile response to the Hughes and Parker nominations by a Senate that was still under nominal Republican control.

Thus, while the efforts of the Roosevelt administration to promote legal realism and the efforts of the Reagan administration to promote originalism both represented efforts to exert influence upon a recalcitrant judiciary by galvanizing public opinion, their effects upon the legal marketplace of ideas differed. As legal realism was already relatively well established in the elite ranks of the legal academy by 1933 and was consistent with broader political and academic currents, calls by Franklin Roosevelt and his surrogates for interpreting the Constitution as a living document, although associated with upsurges in realist scholarship, did not serve the same legitimating function that calls by Ronald Reagan's surrogates for a jurisprudence of original intention did. In order to better understand how legal realism was able to establish itself in this way, it is necessary to look back in greater detail to the Lochner era struggle between the progressive proponents of sociological jurisprudence and the conservative proponents of legal formalism and how this struggle was shaped by the unique political dynamics of the 4th Party System.

CHAPTER 4

Legal Formalism and the 4th Party System's Republican Regime

INTRODUCTION

The period known as the Lochner era has become synonymous with judicial activism and is widely remembered as a period in which a conservative judiciary "felt free to manufacture rights that did not exist and intrude into the legislature's sphere of authority."[1] This style of jurisprudence reflected adherence to a distinctive legal ideology known as legal formalism. Conceptualizing the law as a complete, autonomous, and apolitical system and the judicial process as a process of discovering rather than making the law, legal formalism dovetailed with conservative trends in national politics in the late 19th and early 20th centuries insofar as it also advanced the idea of economic liberty as a constitutional right. This synergy between jurisprudential and political trends became particularly evident in 1895, when the Supreme Court handed down a trilogy of decisions that signaled both its formalism and its conservatism, decisions that construed federal anti-trust legislation in a manner that rendered it largely ineffective, limited the activities of labor unions, and declared the federal income tax unconstitutional. These decisions set the stage for the realigning election of 1896, which pitted a Republican Party that ran on a platform of economic conservatism and expressed its support for the Court and its jurisprudence against a Democratic Party that ran on a platform of economic populism and engaged in the harshest rhetorical attacks on the federal judiciary since the Civil War. Unique among major realignments of the political system in the United States, this contest resulted in a decisive victory for the representatives of the status quo, the Republican defenders of legal formalism. What followed was an intensification of the formalist pattern of jurisprudence that the Court (and courts at the state level) had exhibited. Moreover, this formalism was consistent with the shared "set of beliefs, values, and assumptions about the law and the role of the courts in construing law" that bound the elite ranks of the legal profession together.[2]

This chapter examines the depth and historical provenance of these shared beliefs, values, and assumptions about the law. In particular, it analyzes the temporal relationship between immigration, industrialization, and urbanization and the emergence of destabilizing class conflict, trends in legal education, scholarship, and jurisprudence, public embraces and critiques of legal formalism by political actors associated with the Republican and Democratic parties, and the growth in the amount of formalist scholarship in elite law reviews. It finds that while formalism experienced a significant and sudden upsurge in the legal marketplace of ideas in response to widespread labor strife and the growing political strength of the populist movement during the early 1890s, formalism experienced an equally significant decline when economic conditions improved and the threat of socialism receded. Most importantly, this decline occurred despite the consolidation of the Republican political-electoral regime of the 4th Party System, whose leaders embraced legal formalism and drew frequent contrasts with their Democratic opponents' critiques of the courts. This pattern underscores the divide within this regime between its conservative and progressive factions and illustrates how the intercurrence of contradictory political traditions within political orders and within institutions can also be found in the legal marketplace of ideas. It also contextualizes the rise of the legal realist movement as the successful culmination of a 30-year struggle by progressives to gain control of the legal marketplace of ideas from the traditional conservative legal establishment.

THE RISE OF THE 4TH PARTY SYSTEM'S REPUBLICAN REGIME

The emergence of the 4th Party System was driven by the fading of the issues related to the Civil War and Reconstruction that had defined the 3rd Party System and the rise of a new set of issues related to the role of government in regulating the economy and providing for social welfare. However, although both the issues that animated partisan competition and the composition of partisan coalitions had changed, the 4th Party System represented continuity with the 3rd Party System insofar as the Republican Party remained the nation's majority party (see Table 4.1). Just as Republican candidates had won seven of the nine

Table 4.1: Partisan Control of Political Institutions during the 4th Party System

Congress (Years)	*House of Representatives (Party Breakdown)*	*Senate (Party Breakdown)*	*Presidency (President)*	*Control*
55th (1897-1899)	Republican (206-124-22-3-1-1)	Republican (44-34-5-5-2)	Republican (McKinley)	Complete
56th (1899-1901)	Republican (187-161-5-2-1-1)	Republican (53-26-5-3-2)	Republican (McKinley)	Complete
57th (1901-1903)	Republican (200-151-5-1)	Republican (56-32-2)	Republican (McKinley/T. Roosevelt)	Complete
58th (1903-1905)	Republican (207-176-3)	Republican (57-33)	Republican (T. Roosevelt)	Complete
59th (1905-1907)	Republican (251-135)	Republican (58-32)	Republican (T. Roosevelt)	Complete
60th (1907-1909)	Republican (223-167-1)	Republican (61-31)	Republican (T. Roosevelt)	Complete
61st (1909-1911)	Republican (219-172)	Republican (60-32)	Republican (Taft)	Complete
62nd (1911-1913)	Democratic (230-162-1-1)	Republican (52-44)	Republican (Taft)	Divided
63rd (1913-1915)	Democratic (291-134-9-1)	Democratic (51-44-1)	Democratic (Wilson)	Opposition
64th (1915-1917)	Democratic (230-196-6-1-1-1)	Democratic (56-40)	Democratic (Wilson)	Opposition
65th (1917-1919)	Democratic (214-215-3-1-1-1)	Democratic (54-42)	Democratic (Wilson)	Opposition
66th (1919-1921)	Republican (240-192-1-1)	Republican (49-47)	Democratic (Wilson)	Divided
67th (1921-1923)	Republican (302-131-1-1)	Republican (59-37)	Republican (Harding)	Complete
68th (1923-1925)	Republican (225-207-2-1)	Republican (53-42-1)	Republican (Harding/Coolidge)	Complete
69th (1925-1927)	Republican (247-183-3-1-1)	Republican (54-41-1)	Republican (Coolidge)	Complete
70th (1927-1929)	Republican (238-194-2-1)	Republican (48-46-1)	Republican (Coolidge)	Complete
71st (1929-1931)	Republican (270-164-1)	Republican (56-39-1)	Republican (Hoover)	Complete
72nd (1931-1933)	Democratic (217-217-1)	Republican (48-47-1)	Republican (Hoover)	Divided

presidential elections between 1860 and 1892, Republican candidates would win seven of the nine presidential elections between 1896 and 1928. The Democratic Party was only able to break the Republican lock on the presidency in 1912, when the split between the Republican Party's conservative and progressive factions and former president Theodore Roosevelt's third party candidacy allowed Woodrow Wilson to win the presidency with only 42% of the popular vote, and 1916, when Wilson was narrowly reelected with another popular vote plurality. The 4th Party System's Republican regime was even more dominant than the previous Republican regime in congressional elections. While control of Congress had been closely contested for most of the 3rd Party System, with Republicans simultaneously controlling both houses of Congress for only 18 of the party system's 36 years, the 4th Party System would see the Republican Party enjoy an extended period of dominance in congressional elections that was interrupted only briefly during the Taft and Wilson administrations. This dominance is even more impressive when the results of congressional elections during the 4th Party System are disaggregated by region. Although congressional delegations from the "Solid South" remained almost entirely Democratic, Republicans became nearly as dominant throughout the rest of the country during this period, capturing as many as 90% of non-Southern congressional seats in some elections.[3]

This dominance was rooted in the failed attempt by the Democratic Party to realign the electorate in its favor in the election of 1896. After years of "sham battles that decided no consequential issues," the Democratic Party moved to draw a clearer contrast with the Republicans by aligning itself with the demands of agrarian protest movements and organized labor.[4] However, this turn toward populism failed to gain the party many new supporters among farmers and urban laborers. Northern farmers, seeing Republican support for protective tariffs rather than Democratic support for monetary reform as the answer to their problems, remained loyal to the Republican Party despite the Democrats' agrarian appeals. Even more importantly, Northern cities, whose workers feared the inflationary effects of Democratic monetary policies and were repelled by Democratic presidential nominee William Jennings Bryan's polarizing references to "'your cities' and 'our farms,'" turned decisively toward the Republican Party.[5] With the Democratic Party reduced to its traditional base in the South, Republican candidates won four consecutive presidential elections and Republicans consolidated their hold on Congress.

However, the Republican Party that dominated national politics in the early 20th century was a party divided between its conservative and progressive factions. Although William McKinley had ushered in a new Republican regime by positioning his party as a conservative alternative to the radicalism of William Jennings Bryan and the Democrats, the reformist impulses that had led the Democrats to move to the left would find expression in both parties. This became evident early in the 4th Party System when Theodore Roosevelt assumed the presidency upon McKinley's assassination in 1901. Roosevelt's progressive record as president, which included aggressive enforcement of anti-trust laws, support for organized labor, and new consumer and product safety regulations, was a source of continual tension with conservative party elites and illustrated the ideological heterogeneity of both parties during the 4th Party System. This ideological heterogeneity facilitated the formation of bipartisan coalitions of progressive Republicans and Democrats that succeeded in enacting much of the progressive movement's reform agenda despite continued Republican control of Congress. It also undermined the power of the conservative leadership of the Republican caucus in Congress, culminating in the successful effort by a coalition of progressive Republicans and Democrats to strip Speaker of the House Joseph Cannon of many of his powers as speaker in 1910.[6] These intramural conflicts ultimately cost the Republican Party control of Congress and the presidency. Although William Taft had succeeded Theodore Roosevelt as president with Roosevelt's endorsement, Taft's record aligned more closely with his party's conservative faction and exacerbated ideological tensions within the party. The alienation of progressive Republicans played a major role in the Democrats taking control of the House of Representatives in the 1910 midterm elections and in the Democrats taking control of the White House in the election of 1912, when Theodore Roosevelt's attempt to regain the presidency as the candidate of the Progressive Party doomed Taft's reelection campaign.

The six years of complete Democratic control of the federal government that followed saw the enaction of many policies long championed by progressives as part of Woodrow Wilson's New

Freedom agenda, such as the creation of the Federal Reserve and the passage of anti-trust and child labor legislation. However, the Republican Party regained its normal advantage in congressional and presidential elections once it began to reestablish its unity. After the Republicans reclaimed majorities in both houses of Congress in the 1918 midterm elections, Warren Harding recaptured the presidency for the party in 1920 in what remains the largest popular vote landslide in American history. Indeed, no Democratic presidential nominee won more than 40% of the popular vote between 1920 and 1928. The overwhelming resurgence of the 4th Party System's Republican regime reflected the social and political climate of the 1920s. Not only had the public grown weary of the reformist zeal of the Progressive Era, which lost momentum in a period of unprecedented economic prosperity, it had turned strongly against the internationalist foreign policy of the Wilson administration. These trends placed conservatives more firmly in control of the national Republican Party and led to a resurgence of conservatism in the Democratic Party. This led to what Tucker terms the "high tide of American conservatism" in the presidential election of 1924, in which both Republican candidate Calvin Coolidge and Democratic candidate John Davis campaigned on platforms of limited government and reduced regulation and taxation.[7] Such comity would also characterize the 1928 presidential election, in which Democratic candidate Al Smith went to great lengths to assure voters that he was "safe, sound, and as well liked by business as anyone could desire."[8] The depth of this conservative consensus illustrates the suddenness and thoroughness of the New Deal earthquake that would realign the political system only four years later.

LEGAL FORMALISM AND ITS ORIGINS

The conservative zeitgeist of the 1920s also led to an acceleration of formalist trends in jurisprudence that produced many of the most notable cases of the Lochner era. The most distinctive attribute of the Lochner era of legal formalism was its unprecedented level of judicial activism. This activism was particularly pronounced at the federal level. Whereas the Supreme Court had throughout most of its prior history been quite restrained in its exercise of its power of judicial review, it would invalidate over 200 statutes on individual rights grounds between 1890 and 1937.[9] A majority of these statutes were labor and market regulations that were construed as unconstitutional infringements upon individual rights to freely exchange labor and goods. Cases such as *Lochner v. New York*, in which the Court invalidated legislation restricting the working hours of bakers, and *Coppage v. Kansas*, in which the Court invalidated legislation outlawing yellow dog employment contracts, have come to be viewed as paradigmatic examples of the Court substituting its own policy preferences for those of legislatures. Such decisions mirrored a similar wave of judicial activism at the state level, with the doctrine of economic substantive due process that formed the basis for decisions such as *Lochner* and *Coppage* being articulated by several state supreme courts prior to being embraced by the United States Supreme Court.[10]

However, the formalist turn in jurisprudence was not solely a "defense of conservative economic principles thinly disguised as…constitutional decision" that reflected elite lawyers' anxieties in a time of class conflict.[11] Instead, important precursors to the doctrines that have been associated with legal formalism, such as liberty of contract, can be found in Jacksonian politicians' hostility toward government-sponsored privileges and in the abolitionist movement and the early Republican Party's "definition of freedom as resting on economic independence."[12] Moreover, even earlier precursors to these doctrines can be found in the statements and writings of the framers of the Constitution, who expressed an intent to create a government whose structure would provide safeguards against the ills of factional politics. Thus, legal formalism's antagonism toward laws reordering market relations at the behest of organized labor, farmers, and other special interests can be understood in large part as the application of a "principle of political legitimacy that the framers sought to permanently enshrine in the fundamental law."[13]

Nonetheless, legal formalism did represent a significant departure from the mode of legal discourse that had prevailed for most of the 19th century in several important respects. Reflective of a legal profession that at the time still operated largely through a "fragmentary and disconnected" system of common law writs for bringing and defending different types of legal actions, this older mode of legal discourse was generally functionalist, pragmatic, and utilized a relatively low level of abstraction.[14] For this reason, early efforts by legal formalists to systematize the law were initially met with considerable opposition from the legal profession, which feared that such systematization would "encourage the development of abstract and integrated fields of law that sacrificed professional utility."[15]

More importantly, legal formalism represented not only a stylistic but also a substantive departure from 19th century legal thought. Although precursors to some of the legal doctrines associated with formalism such as liberty of contract can be found in the aforementioned tradition of hostility toward factional politics, the guise that these doctrines took in the late 19th century reflected more recent trends in legal thought. In particular, both the idea of police power as one of a handful of discrete and limited categories of state power and its associated concept of economic substantive due process did not exist prior to the Civil War. Indeed, 19th century legal thought understood police power as a virtually unlimited source of power that allowed state and local governments to promote the people's welfare. Moreover, contrary to the dominant narrative of antebellum America as a nearly stateless society, this power was used liberally throughout the 19th century to promote public health, morality, and safety and to regulate business enterprises.[16] The underpinnings of this "well-regulated society" were consistently reinforced by judicial decisions, such as Justice Samuel Miller's opinion for the Supreme Court in *The Slaughterhouse Cases*, which described police power as a power that "is, and must be from its very nature, incapable of any exact definition or limitation."[17]

Such expansive understandings of police power were part and parcel of the generally flexible and instrumental conception of the law that prevailed for most of the 19th century. This conception of the law was particularly dominant in common law interpretation, where judges enthusiastically embraced the task of transforming the "pre-commercial and anti-developmental" legal doctrines of the 18th century to meet the needs of a rapidly growing and developing nation.[18] Illustrative of this enthusiasm was the willingness of prominent jurists such as Nathaniel Chipman, the chief justice of the Supreme Court of Vermont and the author of several influential treatises, to openly reject the "arbitrary authority of customary rules" and "subservience to precedent" that was "made at a time when the state of society and of property were very different."[19] Consequently, the 19th century was a period of legal innovation in which areas of the law such as commercial law, contracts, and property were revolutionized in what has been described as one of the greatest "creative outbursts of modern legal history."[20] For this reason, legal formalism and its rigid distinction between judging and policymaking has been characterized as a "revolutionary" departure from existing patterns of legal thought, one that sought to "overthrow a regime of governance sanctioned by…centuries of experience."[21]

This revolutionary departure was a product of a historical context distinguished by pervasive social conflict driven by immigration, industrialization, and urbanization. In particular, the politicization of this conflict, which was reflected in increasing political agitation by organized labor and agrarian protest movements, intensified desires among legal scholars and judges for law to provide a "non-political cushion or buffer between state and society."[22] This buffer took the form of the development of more abstract, integrated, and systematic concepts and classifications, concepts and classifications that were intended to make law less political and more scientific, and the development of a sharper distinction between private and public law, one that created an "oasis of private rights free from state interference."[23] This trend toward systematization was reflected in the numerous pioneering efforts of the period to not only produce comprehensive treatises on broad areas of the law, such as contracts and torts, but also to reduce the complexity that had previously characterized these areas of the law to a handful of general principles. These efforts to apply greater scientific rigor to an unsystematized field of study and to draw a clearer distinction between "is" and "ought" were not limited to the legal academy and reflected the general intellectual climate of the period. In particular, they reflected the rise of scientific positivism and utilitarian social philosophy, which represented two of the major intellectual developments of the late 19th century. Emblematic of this rise were the work of natural scientists such as Charles Darwin and Louis Agassiz, both of whom played important roles in advancing the separation of scientific inquiry from religious and philosophical beliefs and in leading the movement toward the inductive approach that is characteristic of modern science, and the work of philosophers such as Charles Peirce, whose philosophy of pragmatism is credited with advancing the idea of empirical truth as something that is immutable, discoverable, and independent of opinion.[24] Consistent with these broader trends, legal discourse was increasingly characterized by the use of bright line classifications that gave the law a scientific air of "certainty and logical inexorability."[25]

This air of certainty and logical inexorability was also increasingly evident in legal education, which underwent a major transformation during this period. This transformation was driven largely by Christopher Langdell's tenure as the dean of Harvard Law School from 1870 to 1895, which saw the development of several mainstays of modern legal education. Not only did Langdell introduce the first casebooks, he also pioneered the use of the case method as a method of instruction. Most importantly, both of these innovations were closely linked to Langdell's strongly formalistic conception of the law. As the preface to Langdell's first casebook, *A Selection of Cases on the Law of Contracts*, states, Langdell's view was that law should be "considered as a science," a science that "consists of certain principles or doctrines" that can be "traced in the main through a series of cases."[26] This was a view that was shared by most of the members of Harvard Law School's faculty, which included prominent formalists such as James Barr Ames and Joseph Beale. Consequently, Harvard Law School became known as the center of formalist pedagogy and thought. These formalist underpinnings made the case method an "effective technique of indoctrination, socialization, and ideological regimentation" that contributed to the entrenchment of formalist modes of discourse and thought in the legal profession.[27] This entrenchment was aided by the rapid adoption of the case method by other law schools, which responded to concerted lobbying on its behalf by Harvard Law School's influential network of alumni and to the appeal of the increased intellectual demands that it made of law students.[28] Moreover, the "Harvardization" of legal education extended beyond widespread adoption of the case method and by the 1920s most law schools had also adopted Harvard's three-year course, its practice of hiring full-time law professors rather than practitioners, and its core curriculum, which was limited to purely legal subjects and jettisoned the courses in political science and philosophy that had once been staples of law school curricula.[29] Like the case method, these innovations contributed to legal education's move away from its historic emphasis on practical training and to the ascendancy of formalism.

THE OPENING OF THE LOCHNER ERA OF JURISPRUDENCE

The turn toward formalism was reflected not only in legal education, discourse, and thought but most of all in jurisprudence construing the scope of state police power. In this respect state courts were a leading indicator of jurisprudential trends, embracing legal formalism at a time when the Supreme Court remained resistant to the doctrines associated with it and then largely abandoning it in the face of political backlash at a time when the Supreme Court was still in its most activist phase.[30] Indeed, the case that "opened the era" of economic substantive due process was the New York Court of Appeals' 1885 decision in *In re Jacobs*, in which the Court ruled that legislation prohibiting the manufacture of cigars in tenement houses unconstitutionally "interfered with the profitable use of real property" insofar as it denied its owner due process of law by "arbitrarily depriv[ing] him of his property and of some portion of his personal liberty."[31] Within a year the logic underlying this decision had been embraced by the high courts of Illinois, Massachusetts, and Pennsylvania, setting the stage for an unprecedented wave of state court activism that would last until the turn of the 20th century.[32]

Such activism initially found little support on the Supreme Court. Early police power cases had seen the Supreme Court consistently defer judgment on the reasonableness of regulatory legislation to state legislatures and decline to give the Due Process Clause a substantive reading. Thus, the Court held in *The Slaughterhouse Cases* that the 14th Amendment's Privileges and Immunities Clause does not restrict states' police powers and declared in *Munn v. Illinois* that "[f]or protection against abuses by legislatures, the people must resort to the polls, not to the courts."[33] Delivered in 1873 and 1877, respectively, these decisions were emblematic of a legal ideology that was at odds with unfolding trends in legal thought and would soon find itself in the minority on the Court. This turn was publicly anticipated by Justice David Davis, who shortly after leaving the Court in 1877 spoke of the profound transformation in outlook that was taking place on the Court. According to Davis, who warned that "[i]f we lose the courts, we lose all," this transformation reflected the "corrupting influence...of corporate power" and the realization of "corporations'... plans to gain complete control of the Supreme Court."[34]

This transformation became evident when the Court delivered a number of decisions in the 1880s and 1890s that jettisoned this restrained approach to police power cases in favor of a more activist one that enforced the laissez faire constitutionalism integral to legal formalism. The case that has often been identified as the major turning point in this regard was the Court's 1890 decision in *Chicago, Milwaukee & St. Paul Railway Company v. Minnesota*, which effectively overruled *Munn v. Illinois* and its doctrine of deference to railroad and other corporate rates set by state commissions and replaced it with a regime under which courts would be the primary arbiters of the reasonableness and constitutionality of such regulations. This doctrinal change occurred in the context of a period of unprecedented economic distress for farmers that was caused by declining agricultural prices and rising railroad rates and played an important role in precipitating the rise of agrarian protest movements across the Great Plains and the South. These protest movements championed a host of measures considered radical at the time, such as state ownership of railroads and utilities and the abolition of national banks, and their growing political influence led conservatives such as Supreme Court Justice Stephen Field to warn of a coming "war of the poor against the rich."[35] Decisions such as the Minnesota rate case were also significant insofar as they represented the first steps in a "fateful transition from the non-controversial tradition of procedural due process to a substantive reading of the clause."[36]

While the Minnesota rate case drew the ire of agrarian protest movements, it was merely a precursor to the three landmark decisions that the Court handed down in 1895, decisions that would make the Court and its jurisprudence a source of political controversy in a way that it had not been since the period leading up to the Civil War. In *United States v. E.C. Knight Company*, the Court interpreted congressional power under the Constitution to regulate interstate commerce narrowly and in a manner that severely limited the application of federal anti-trust legislation. Specifically, the Court held that manufacturing is a local activity distinct from commerce and therefore not subject to federal regulation. Given the strong public sentiment against "robber barons" and in favor of federal action against cartels and monopolies that existed at the time, sentiment that was reflected in the Sherman Anti-Trust Act being passed unanimously in the House of Representatives and with only a single dissenting vote in the Senate, this decision proved highly controversial.[37] While the Court's evisceration of the Sherman Anti-Trust Act was criticized for its literalistic formalism, the Court's subsequent decision in *In re Debs* would give rise to charges that the Court's formalism was merely camouflage for the conservative politics of its members. Whereas the Court had previously held that a single manufacturer's control of more than 98% of the nation's sugar production was beyond the reach of federal anti-trust legislation, the Court now approved the use of the same legislation to bring criminal charges against labor leaders for organizing a strike in defiance of an injunction, setting the stage for the widespread use of the injunction as a tool against the labor movement. In the same vein, the Court's decision invalidating the federal income tax in *Pollock v. Farmers' Loan & Trust Company*, in which the Court declared that "the Constitution intended to prevent an attack upon accumulated property by mere force of numbers," reflected a similar adherence to formalism and was widely perceived as a "class-oriented decision."[38] This perception was fueled by the fact that the decision reversed precedent that the Court had unanimously established only 14 years earlier in *Springer v. United States* and followed a heated congressional debate on the passage of the Income Tax Act of 1894 in which both sides accused the other of engaging in class warfare.[39]

THE POLITICAL DYNAMICS OF LEGAL FORMALISM

These decisions achieved particular notoriety due to the important roles that President Grover Cleveland and his administration played in the events leading up to them. Not only had Attorney General Richard Olney instructed United States attorneys to obtain injunctions against striking railroad employees, he subsequently instructed them to obtain indictments against Eugene Debs and other labor leaders when these injunctions were violated, culminating in the Court's decision in *In re Debs* approving labor injunctions. Moreover, Olney's "weak presentation" of the federal government's case in *United States v. E.C. Knight Company* has been attributed to the Cleveland administration's lukewarm support for the Sherman Anti-Trust Act, a lack of support evidenced by the fact that Olney later "indicated he was pleased with the outcome" in the case.[40] These actions contributed to the courts becoming a prominent issue in the 1896 presidential election. Indeed, as Burnham observes, the extent to which the courts were a driving force behind the political realignment that followed represented a "metapolitical ascendancy…within the whole American political system" for the judiciary that has "never [been] seen before or since."[41]

The newfound political salience of the courts was also the product of more than a decade of social unrest known as the "age of anxiety."[42] This unrest stemmed largely from persistent conflict between labor and management that gave rise to periodic episodes of "widespread strikes, accompanied by scores of deaths, arson, and insurrection in…the nation's major cities" and to a "wave of anti-communist hysteria."[43] These eruptions of class conflict, which included incidents such as the Great Railroad Strike of 1877, the Haymarket massacre of 1886, and the Pullman strike of 1894, were a reflection of the rapid pace of American industrialization and urbanization following the Civil War. They were also a consequence of an unprecedented period of economic deflation and low growth known as the "long-wave depression" that began with the Panic of 1873 and did not end until 1897.[44] Moreover, these incidents were merely the most prominent in a protracted conflict that directly affected millions of workers. For example, there were over 10,000 strikes and lockouts nationwide during the 1880s and over 400,000 workers went on strike during the national strike of 1886 alone.[45]

This intensification of class conflict contributed to an intensification of formalist trends in legal thought. This is evident in the rhetoric used by leading members of the legal profession, whose views on the law were increasingly shaped by the rising threat of the poor "lash[ing] out in an expropriating frenzy to seize the accumulations of the rich."[46] For example, John Dillon, the president of the American Bar Association, warned of the dire threat to property posed by a "proletariat armed with the ballot in one hand and a gun in the other" while Tiedeman's influential *Treatise on the Limitations of Police Power in the United States* prefaces its discussion of these limitations with an ominous warning that "socialism, communism, and anarchism are rampant throughout the civilized world."[47] Such rhetoric was also used by the members of the Supreme Court, who in their statements off the bench regularly presented the Court and its jurisprudence as bulwarks against class conflict. For example, Justice David Brewer's 1893 speech to the New York State Bar Association defended restrictions placed by the Court upon the "improper use of labor organizations" and the legislative regulation of fees in property subjected to public uses as necessary to prevent more "direct effort[s] on the part of the many to seize the property of the few" while Justice Stephen Field declared in an 1890 speech commemorating the Court's centennial that "as the inequalities in the conditions of men become more and more marked…it becomes more and more the imperative duty of the Supreme Court to enforce every guarantee of the Constitution."[48] Such views reflected the fact that the elite ranks of the legal profession had historically been a deeply conservative force in American life. As Wiecek explains, there was a tradition of "open hostility between the better kinds of lawyers and the impulses of the masses," a tradition reinforced by a cultural divide within the legal profession between the "W.A.S.P. elite" that dominated the corporate bar and the legal academy and the "nouveaux…attorneys" who tended to represent individual clients, attorneys who often came from immigrant backgrounds and were more likely to have received their legal training through apprenticeships than at university law schools.[49] This divide was increasingly reinforced by the enaction of more restrictive law school admissions policies. For example, Harvard Law School began to require that prospective students hold a bachelor's degree from an accredited college or university in the 1890s, a policy that was widely accused of "exclud[ing] all but a privileged class from admission to the practice of law."[50]

However, the class conflict that defined this period in American history initially found little expression in national politics as the leaders of both the Democratic and Republican parties were united in their economic conservatism. Indeed, the Democratic Cleveland administration distinguished itself by its particular hostility toward the labor movement, not only pursuing injunctive relief in federal court to end the Pullman Strike but also subsequently dispatching federal troops to Chicago and 20 other rail centers to break the strike when litigation failed. Indicative of the lack of any real differences between the leadership of the two major parties on the economic issues of the day, these actions received broad bipartisan support from most of the nation's leading newspapers.[51] Moreover, political elites in both parties also shared a common legal ideology. Grover Cleveland's judicial nominees were largely indistinguishable from Republican judicial nominees.[52] Indeed, Cleveland would give the Supreme Court its most consistent supporter of the doctrine of economic substantive due process with his nomination of Rufus Peckham, the author of *Lochner v. New York*. Thus, rather than partisan, the most significant cleavage on the Court was generational, with the cohort of justices appointed in the 1860s and 70s by Abraham Lincoln, Ulysses Grant, and Rutherford Hayes generally exhibiting greater deference to regulatory legislation than the cohort of justices appointed in the 1880s and 90s by James Garfield, Chester Arthur, Benjamin Harrison, and Grover Cleveland. Whereas the former were distinguished primarily by their concern with maintaining a balance between state and federal power, the latter were distinguished primarily by their concern with protecting property rights from state or federal power.[53]

This era of partisan convergence would come to an end in the face of deteriorating economic conditions in the early 1890s. The economic downturn known as the Panic of 1893 represented the most severe economic downturn that the United States had experienced prior to the Great Depression. Its effects were particularly felt among the urban working class as unemployment in the manufacturing sector reached 50% by 1894, fueling the increasing radicalization of the labor movement.[54] The continued economic conservatism of both major parties in the face of this crisis contributed to the rise of the People's Party, whose members were known as the Populists, as a significant political force. Growing out of the agrarian protest movements that had emerged in response to recurring farmer's debt crises, the party gave voice to those dissatisfied with the economic conservatism of the Democratic and Republican parties, advocating a host of progressive measures such as a national eight-hour workday, a graduated income tax, and state ownership of railroads and utilities.[55] Capturing the electoral votes of four states in the 1892 presidential election as well as several governorships and a substantial number of congressional and state legislative seats, the Populists were largely co-opted and absorbed by the Democrats after the progressive supporters of William Jennings Bryan seized control of the Democratic Party from the conservative supporters of Grover Cleveland at the party's 1896 national convention. This hostile takeover of the Democratic Party would give rise to a major realignment of the political system as Bryan's nomination led substantial numbers of conservative Democrats to leave the party, whose move to the left simultaneously attracted a smaller number of progressive Republicans.

As has historically been the case in realigning elections in which the constitutional order is threatened with reconstruction by a popular insurgency, a Supreme Court that was strongly identified with the values and commitments of the existing political-electoral regime would feature as a major issue in the election of 1896. This was reflected in the fact that the Democrats flaunted their hostility to the Court and its jurisprudence at every opportunity during the campaign. Not only did the party platform criticize the Court's decisions declaring the federal income tax unconstitutional and approving the labor injunction, which it branded a "new and highly dangerous form of oppression…in contempt of the laws of states and rights of citizens," its reference to "the Court as it may hereafter be constituted" was widely recognized as an implicit embrace of proposals to pack the Court. The relatively large amount of space devoted to attacks on the judiciary in the platform was a prelude to the extensive anti-judicial rhetoric used in the subsequent campaign by William Jennings Bryan and his surrogates, who denounced "government by injunction" and the courts "becom[ing] at once legislators, judges, and executioners."[56] Bryan's statements regarding the courts also indicated a realist conception of the judicial process that rejected formalist conceptions of the courts as an apolitical institution, noting that "the Supreme Court changes from time to time" and that "future judges may adhere to the precedents of a hundred years, instead of adhering to a decision rendered by a majority of one."[57] In contrast, Republican Party nominee William McKinley and his surrogates consistently defended the Court and its jurisprudence. Typical of these defenses was former president Benjamin Harrison's speech commending the "high-minded, independent judiciary" for "hold[ing]…the line on questions between wealth and labor, between the rich and poor."[58] The Republicans also chided the Democrats for politicizing the courts, denouncing the Democrats' rhetoric as an "assault upon our constitutional form of government" and accusing the Democrats of "prostituting the power and duty of the…courts" by making overt "threat[s] to pack the Supreme Court of the United States."[59]

These exchanges were a microcosm of the tone of the campaign as a whole, in which Bryan's perceived radicalism was a major factor contributing to his defeat. This defeat transformed the political system from one that had a close partisan balance to one in which the Republicans were the clear majority party. As Sundquist explains, this was the result of the fact that the realignment that occurred was "largely a one-way movement" of conservative Northern Democrats leaving the party.[60] The comparative unwillingness of progressive

Republicans to cross party lines in the opposite direction is illustrative of the enduring legacy of the Civil War and its tainting of the Democratic label outside of the South, factors that made it "too great an emotional and psychological strain" for these voters to become Democrats.[61] Consequently, although the Republican majority that emerged from the election of 1896 has been associated with laissez faire economics and legal formalism, it contained a large progressive faction inclined toward alternative conceptions of the law and its interpretation.

This faction was bolstered by the fact that most of the Populists who had defected from the Republican Party in the early 1890s quietly returned to the Republican fold following the election of 1896, their cultural and historical reasons for doing so encapsulated by Senator William Peffer's declaration that he had "always been against the Democrats."[62] It was also bolstered by the assassination of William McKinley and his replacement by Theodore Roosevelt, whose charismatic leadership during his seven and a half years as president did much to sustain and encourage Republican progressivism. This encouragement played an important role in progressives taking and maintaining control of the Republican parties of key states such as California and New York and of several Midwestern states during the Roosevelt administration.[63] Moreover, although conservatives maintained control of the national Republican Party throughout the 4th Party System, coalitions of progressive Republicans and Democrats nonetheless made possible the major pieces of legislation and the constitutional amendments that gave the Progressive Era its name. These included the Keating-Owen Act outlawing child labor, the Pure Food and Drug Act providing for food and product safety, and the Federal Reserve Act reforming the banking and monetary systems and the 16th, 17th, 18th, and 19th amendments to the United States Constitution, which provided for the federal income tax, direct election of senators, Prohibition, and women's suffrage.

UNDERSTANDING THE RELATIONSHIP BETWEEN THE POLITICAL TRIUMPH OF CONSERVATISM AND THE FORMALIST TURN IN LEGAL THOUGHT

As a period of political realignment in which legal thought and jurisprudence underwent a significant transformation that mirrored realigning trends in electoral politics, the 1890s present a number of parallels to the 1930s and 1980s. In order to measure the timing and magnitude of the formalist turn in legal thought and assess its relationship to the increasing politicization of issues relating to legal and constitutional interpretation, an analysis of the number of formalist and anti-formalist publications appearing in the two most influential law reviews over a ten-year period bracketing the realigning election of 1896 was conducted.

Legal formalism was defined in terms of both the general conception of the nature of law and the judicial process that it has come to be associated with and in terms of the specific legal doctrines that it gave rise to. Specifically, formalist publications were defined as publications that describe the law as a complete and autonomous system of neutral principles and the judicial process as the scientific and apolitical process of applying these principles to concrete cases. For example, these included Bailey's article declaring that "law is a science," one that is "based on rules and principles which we can…carry out to their logical results" and Tiedeman's article declaring that "law is not made by the courts" and that "[t]he judge is but an instrument for [its] promulgation."[64] Formalist publications also included publications that apply this conception of the nature of law and the judicial process and its tendency toward bright line principles to the major issue that confronted courts in the late 19th and early 20th centuries: the conflict between state powers of eminent domain, regulation, and taxation and individual rights to contract and property. Thus, formalist publications included publications embracing the right to liberty of contract in relatively absolutist terms, such as Hayden's article characterizing legislation establishing an eight-hour workday as unconstitutional "governmental paternalism…carried to an almost unlimited degree" as well as publications advancing narrow and formalistic constructions of the scope of state power in other areas of the law.[65] For example, these included Foster's article arguing in favor of a bright line delineation of state power over property affected with a public interest, which asserts that "[i]f the final word as to what is or what is not within the scope of the police power be left to a legislative majority, all security to the citizen is gone; all he has…would be subject to the veto or the regulation of the omnipotent half plus one," and Yeaman's article advocating more active judicial enforcement of constitutional limitations on state police power, which asserts that the "only…legitimate function of government is to protect the individual in his life, liberty, person, property, reputation, and contractual rights."[66]

Anti-formalist publications fell primarily into two categories. The first of these included publications that critique legal formalism's general conception of the nature of law and the judicial process, arguing that this conception fails to accord with reality and that it has negative practical implications. For example, these included Holmes's article arguing that the "true science of the law does not consist mainly in a theological working out of dogma or a logical development as in mathematics" and Russell's more direct attack on the "extravagant pretensions put forth by enthusiastic writers as to the nature and scope of the law."[67] These also included publications describing the deleterious effects of legal formalism on the functioning of the legal system, such as Smith's article arguing that the result of formalism's permeation of legal culture and discourse was "courts attempt[ing] to lay down hard and fast rules…which it has been impossible to adhere to" and subsequently being forced to make strenuous "efforts…to conceal the fact that the law [is] being altered by their decisions."[68] Anti-formalist publications also included critiques of the specific legal doctrines associated with legal formalism, such as the doctrine of liberty of contract. For example, these included Hadley's article critiquing these doctrines as being "based on assumptions…which may have been approximately true in the 18th century but are totally false in the 19th" and Whitney's attack on them as embodying a troubling trend of "courts attempt[ing] to interpose their opinions on matters of policy" in a way that "…disarrange[s] our system of government."[69]

A total of 1,940 articles, book reviews, comments, and notes were published in the two law reviews that were analyzed during the time period under consideration. A total of 100 of these publications were coded as formalist and a total of 59 of these publications were coded as anti-formalist. The annual numbers of formalist and anti-formalist publications are expressed as percentages of the total number of articles, book reviews, comments, and notes appearing each year in these law reviews. It was anticipated that significant increases in the number of formalist publications would follow closely on the heels of the success of the Populists in the 1892 elections and the Panic of 1893, both of which brought the issue of the role of the state in regulating the economy to the fore and raised the specter of class warfare, and the 1896 presidential election, in which the Republican Party triumphed by embracing legal formalism and attacking its Democratic opponents as a threat to the rule of law. It was also anticipated that the number of formalist publications would remain relatively stable in the years following the 1896 presidential election as the political-electoral regime that emerged from the election was consolidated during a period of economic prosperity in which legal formalism receded as a political issue. Conversely, it was anticipated that the number of anti-formalist publications would increase significantly following the Democratic Party's 1896 embrace of critiques of legal formalism that had previously only been articulated by the Populists and other third parties on the margins of American politics but that this growth would lose momentum following the failure of the Bryan campaign.

The results indicate a waxing and waning of legal formalism in the legal marketplace of ideas during the time period analyzed that is consistent with some of these expectations and inconsistent with others. While anti-formalist publications were initially as common as formalist publications, formalist perspectives came to dominate the legal marketplace of ideas between 1893 and 1896. However, the climate of the legal marketplace of ideas began to change once more in the late 1890s and early 1900s as the proportion of formalist publications declined in each subsequent year while the proportion of anti-formalist publications increased in each subsequent year (see Figure 4.1). This pattern is consistent with expectations insofar as it indicates that a major catalyst for the rise of formalism in the legal academy was the labor strife and agrarian radicalism of the early 1890s, which "fueled fears among conservative lawyers of imminent socialism or worse."[70] As the data indicate, these fears became particularly real in 1893. Not only had the Populists suddenly emerged as the most successful third party since the Republicans in the previous fall's elections, the Panic of 1893 had fueled confrontations between labor and management that were unprecedented in both their scope and their level of violence. Thus, whereas "[p]rior to the 1892 election, conservatives did not seem all that concerned about the prospect of an agrarian takeover," such a takeover appeared to be a real possibility less than a year later, one that called for the enlistment of the law and the courts to combat the dangers of populism.[71]

In contrast and contrary to expectations, the Republican Party's embrace of legal formalism appears not to have had any positive impact upon legal discourse. Indeed, the results indicate that the emergence of legal formalism as a partisan issue in 1896 and the articulation of anti-formalist arguments by prominent political actors associated with the Democratic Party primarily had the opposite effect of legitimating anti-formalism in the legal academy. Moreover, this effect, contrary to expectations, was not fleeting but rather laid the groundwork for sustained growth in the amount of anti-formalist scholarship. This

Figure 4.1: Legal Formalist and Anti-Formalist Publications Appearing in the 2 most Influential Law Reviews, 1891-1901

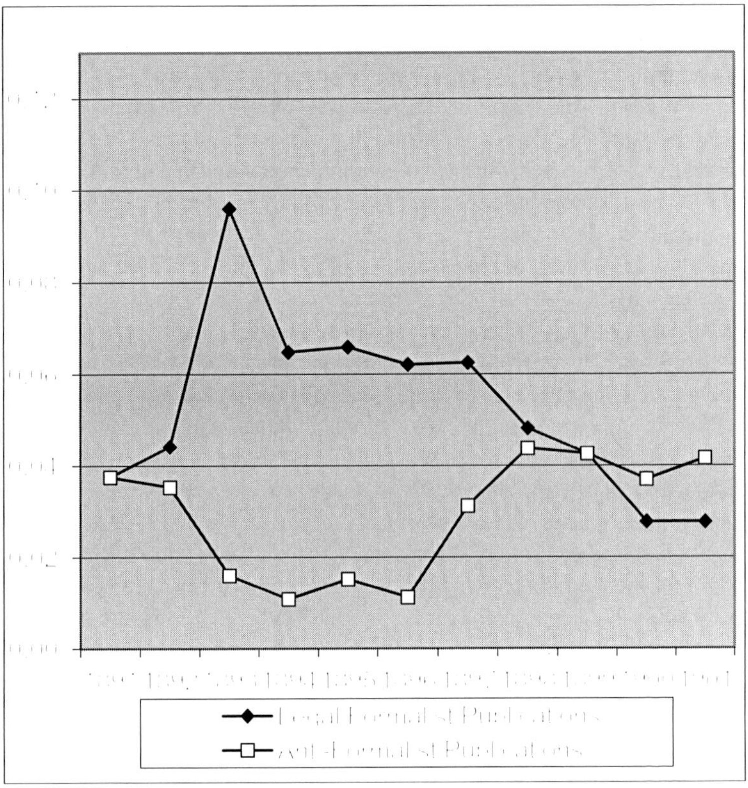

somewhat paradoxical effect reflects the unique dynamics of the realignment that gave rise to the 4th Party System, which represents the only major realignment of the political system in which the "organized popular forces demanding major change were defeated in their appeals to the national public."[72] For this reason, the Democratic Party's challenge to legal formalism has been termed a "constitutional false positive" insofar as, apart from its ultimate failure, it presents all of the elements of the transformative moments of politically driven legal and constitutional change that Ackerman has termed "constitutional moments."[73] Thus, despite the fact that the opponents of legal formalism failed in their effort to capture the presidency, their arguments would nonetheless gain enduring resonance in the legal academy, helping to set the stage in the short term for the emergence of sociological jurisprudence in the 1900s and in the long term for the emergence of the legal realist movement in the 1920s. Indeed, it was in the years immediately following the election of 1896 that many of the scholars most closely associated with sociological jurisprudence, such as Roscoe Pound and Joseph Bingham, would begin their academic careers.

This resonance also indicates the potential for dissonance between trends in legal scholarship and trends in jurisprudence. In particular, whereas formalism was already on the decline in the elite ranks of the legal academy by the late 1890s, its entrenchment in the rank and file of the legal profession through the case method and other formalistic aspects of legal education meant that it had yet to reach its heyday in the courts. Although decisions such as *United States v. E.C. Knight Company*, *In re Debs*, and *Pollock v. Farmers' Loan & Trust Company* had provided indications of the shape of things to come, the liberty of contract decisions that would define the Lochner era had yet to be delivered as it was not until 1897 that the Court first formally articulated the doctrine of liberty of contract in *Allgeyer v. Louisiana*. Indeed, the even more activist posture that the Court adopted after 1896 has been characterized as a direct reaction to the radical rhetoric of the Bryan campaign.[74]

This activism was also a reflection of conservative control of federal judicial nominations during the 4th Party System. Of the 21 appointments to the Supreme Court that were made between 1896 and 1932, 15 were made by conservatives William McKinley, William Taft, Warren Harding, Calvin Coolidge, and Herbert Hoover while only six were made by progressives Theodore Roosevelt and Woodrow Wilson. Thus, although the progressive anti-formalism represented by justices such as Roosevelt appointee Oliver Wendell Holmes and

Wilson appointee Louis Brandeis was a significant force in American politics and an increasingly significant strain of legal thought, it was a strain of legal thought that was severely underrepresented on the Court due to continued control of the national Republican Party by its conservative faction.

This underrepresentation was also a product of the success of conservative presidents in selecting nominees who shared their constitutional values. Unlike the supply-side problem faced by Republican presidents in the early years of the New Right regime and, to a lesser extent, Democratic presidents in the early years of the New Deal regime, conservative Republican presidents were not encumbered in their ability to appoint reliably conservative Supreme Court justices for most of the duration of the 4th Party System. This reflected not only the ascendancy of formalism in the elite ranks of the legal profession but also the political dominance of the Republican Party, particularly the fact that the Senate was under Republican control for all but six years of the 4th Party System. Consequently, every Supreme Court nominee put forth by a Republican president during this period faced confirmation in a Republican-controlled Senate and with the exception of John Parker all were confirmed. In contrast, the progressive Republican and Democratic presidents that served during this period were encumbered in their ability to appoint reliably progressive Supreme Court justices. Not only did the formalist conception of the law shared by most elite lawyers make identifying qualified progressive nominees difficult, securing confirmation for such nominees also often proved difficult. For example, Woodrow Wilson's nomination of Louis Brandeis was vigorously opposed by the American Bar Association and other legal professional organizations and generated such controversy that the Senate Judiciary Committee was moved to hold public hearings on a judicial nomination for the first time in its history. However, this pattern would eventually reverse as the anti-formalist critiques of the proponents of sociological jurisprudence and legal realism gained traction in the legal profession. In order to illustrate this dynamic, measures of the ideology of all of the justices appointed during the 4th Party System, which are based upon Schmidhauser's ideological typology, are reported in Table 4.2.

That formalism was already strongly entrenched in the legal profession prior to the construction of the 4th Party System's Republican regime is reflected in the fact that nearly all of the justices appointed by William McKinley and William Taft established strongly conservative records on the Court that reflected the regime's formalist legal ideology. Not only were Joseph McKenna, Horace Lurton, Willis Van Devanter, Joseph Lamar, and Mahlon Pitney consistent supporters of the doctrine of economic substantive due process, they also generally embraced a narrow and formalist construction of federal regulatory power under the Interstate Commerce and Taxing and Spending clauses. Thus, their confirmation allowed the Court to expand upon the precedent it laid down in *Lochner v. New York* in cases such as *Adair v. United States* and *Coppage v. Kansas*, which saw the Court invalidate statutes at both the federal and state levels that outlawed yellow dog employment contracts, and *Adkins v. Children's Hospital*, in which the Court declared federal minimum wage legislation unconstitutional. It also allowed the Court to expand upon the precedent it laid down in *United States v. E.C. Knight Company* in cases such as *Hammer v. Dagenhart*, in which the Court held that as manufacturing is distinct from commerce, federal legislation outlawing the sale of goods produced by child labor was not a valid exercise of congressional power to regulate interstate commerce.

The sole exception to this pattern was Charles Evans Hughes, who during both his first and second stints on the Court established a moderately progressive record that diverged considerably from the records of the other justices appointed by conservative Republican presidents and that mirrored his record as governor of New York and as the longtime leader of the progressive faction of the state's Republican Party.[75] In particular, Hughes, despite the fact that many progressives would later oppose his confirmation as chief justice in 1930, was a consistent opponent of the doctrine of economic substantive due process, dissenting in *Coppage* and other cases invalidating regulatory legislation that interfered with the liberty of contract and declaring in his majority opinion in *Chicago, Burlington & Quincy Railroad Company v. McGuire* that "freedom of contract is a qualified and not an absolute right" and that the state may interfere "where the parties do not stand upon an equality."[76] Hughes also embraced a reading of federal regulatory power under the Interstate Commerce Clause that was quite expansive for its time, declaring in his majority opinion in *Houston, East & West Texas Railway Company v. United States* that federal authority "embraces the right to control ...operations in all matters having a close and substantial relationship to interstate traffic."[77]

While William McKinley and William Taft were nonetheless generally successful in using Supreme Court appointments to consolidate the Court's formalist majority, the records of Theodore Roosevelt and Woodrow Wilson in using Supreme Court appointments to move the Court in the opposite direction were more uneven. On the one hand, Oliver Wendell Holmes and Louis Brandeis quickly emerged as the intellectual leaders and core of the Court's anti-formalist bloc, a bloc that usually included William Moody and John Clarke during their relatively brief tenures on the Court. However, on the other hand, the impact that the appointment of these progressives had upon the Court's ideological balance was undermined by the concurrent appointment of two justices (William Day and James McReynolds) who established conservative records on the Court that were inconsistent with the expectations of the presidents that nominated them.[78] Day's majority opinion in *Hammer v. Dagenhart*, which held that federal legislation outlawing the sale of goods produced by child labor was not only outside of the scope of congressional power to regulate interstate commerce but also violated the 10th Amendment insofar as it involved a purely local matter wholly beyond the reach of federal authority, particularly infuriated progressives who had long been disappointed by his jurisprudence. Day also proved to be the swing vote in a number of other important cases in which the Court rejected federal claims of regulatory authority, such as *The Employers' Liability Cases*, which saw federal legislation regulating common carriers that Theodore Roosevelt had actively promoted and signed into law declared unconstitutional. However, Roosevelt's miscalculation in nominating Day, whose judicial philosophy has been described as idiosyncratic and "curiously ambivalent," paled in comparison to Wilson's miscalculation in nominating McReynolds, who quickly emerged as the Court's most conservative justice and its leading proponent of substantive due process.[79] Although his record as Wilson's "trust-busting" attorney general had led Wilson to believe that he would be a progressive voice on the Court, McReynolds has instead been remembered by history primarily as the "most strident Court critic of [Franklin] Roosevelt's New Deal programs."[80] This pattern would persist through the early 1920s as Warren Harding was quite successful in using Supreme Court nominations to prevent the anti-formalist sentiments that were gaining strength in the legal academy and profession from gaining greater representation on the Court.

Table 4.2: Supreme Court Appointments during the 4th Party System

Name	*Appointed*	*President*	*Ideology*	*Born*	*Admitted to Bar*
Joseph McKenna	1898	McKinley	Conservative	1843	1865
Oliver Wendell Holmes	1902	T. Roosevelt	Progressive	1841	1866
William Day	1903	T. Roosevelt	Conservative	1849	1872
William Moody	1906	T. Roosevelt	Progressive	1853	1876
Horace Lurton	1909	Taft	Conservative	1844	1867
Charles Evans Hughes	1910	Taft	Progressive	1862	1884
Willis Van Devanter	1910	Taft	Conservative	1859	1881
Joseph Lamar	1910	Taft	Conservative	1857	1878
Mahlon Pitney	1912	Taft	Conservative	1858	1882
James McReynolds, 1914	Wilson, Conservative	1862	1884		
Louis Brandeis	1916	Wilson	Progressive	1856	1878
John Clarke	1916	Wilson	Progressive	1857	1878
William Taft	1921	Harding	Conservative	1857	1880
George Sutherland	1922	Harding	Conservative	1862	1883
Pierce Butler	1922	Harding	Conservative	1866	1888
Edward Sanford	1923	Harding	Conservative	1865	1889
Harlan Stone	1925	Coolidge	Progressive	1872	1898
Charles Evans Hughes	1930	Hoover	Progressive	1862	1884
Owen Roberts	1930	Hoover	Conservative	1875	1898
Benjamin Cardozo	1932	Hoover	Progressive	1870	1891

However, it appears that there was a change in the dynamics of the supply-side problem as the 4th Party System neared its end. Whereas theretofore it had been progressive presidents who were confronted with this problem, henceforth it would be conservative presidents. This was reflected in the fact that Calvin Coolidge and Herbert Hoover would be somewhat unexpectedly responsible for appointing some of the Court's leading progressives and for moving the Lochner Court in a more liberal direction.[81] These progressives included Harlan Stone, Coolidge's sole appointment to the Court, and Benjamin Cardozo, who was appointed seven years later by Hoover, both of whom would join with Louis Brandeis to form the "three musketeers," the Court's pro-New Deal bloc during Franklin Roosevelt's first term clashes with the Court.[82]

Moreover, the other justices that Hoover named to the Court, Charles Evans Hughes and Owen Roberts, would establish centrist records that stood apart from the formalist tendencies of most of William McKinley, William Taft, and Warren Harding's appointees. This despite the fact that Hoover's political and constitutional values were largely indistinguishable from those of McKinley, Taft, and Harding. Although Hughes's relatively progressive record during his first stint on the Court proved to be a reliable indicator of how he would vote as chief justice and although Cardozo's own anti-formalism was well known as a result of his authorship of *The Nature of the Judicial Process* and of other writings promoting sociological jurisprudence, the records of both Stone and Roberts were rather unexpected. As Galston explains, "liberals viewed Stone with suspicion when President Coolidge appointed him to the Court because of his Republican Party and big business affiliations" while conservatives were confident that he would bolster the Court's formalist majority.[83] Indeed, Chief Justice Taft had lobbied Coolidge on Stone's behalf, assuring Coolidge that Stone "share[d] his preferences."[84] Conversely, members of the budding legal realist movement criticized Stone's tenure as the dean of Columbia Law School, a tenure that had led university president Nicholas Murray Butler to publicly conclude that "legal education had fallen into the ruts."[85] These assessments were largely based upon a series of lectures that Stone had delivered as dean, lectures that suggested support for the doctrine of economic substantive due process and a formalist conception of the law.[86] Similar miscalculation surrounded the nomination of Owen Roberts. Although Roberts was perceived at the time of his nomination as an "economic reactionary" and a "spite nomination" on the part of President Hoover following the Senate's rejection of John Parker, his actual record on the Court was that of a swing voter who was far from the doctrinaire formalist that critics of his nomination feared he would be.[87]

The fact that Republican presidents in the waning years of the 4th Party System found it increasingly difficult not only to secure Senate confirmation of Supreme Court nominees identified with legal formalism but also to identify nominees who would be reliable formalists on the bench indicates that a significant generational shift had occurred. In particular, the generation of lawyers from which unexpectedly progressive justices such as Chief Justice Stone and Justice Roberts were drawn was the generation that had received its legal training in the latter half of the 1890s, a period in which the tide of opinion was beginning to turn against legal formalism in the elite ranks of the legal academy. In contrast, their immediate predecessors were drawn largely from the generation that had received its legal education in the 1870s and 1880s, a period in which legal formalism was beginning to entrench itself in the legal academy through changes in law school curricula and pedagogy and in which widespread social unrest generated strong support for legal formalism among many elite lawyers.

These jurisprudential cleavages among Republican appointees also provide support for the conclusions of a substantial body of revisionist scholarship that has challenged the dominant characterization of the 4th Party System as a period of untrammeled formalism in legal thought and jurisprudence.[88] This body of scholarship has demonstrated that legal formalism's hegemony in the legal marketplace of ideas during this period has been overstated and that anti-formalist critiques that are often attributed to proponents of sociological jurisprudence and the legal realist movement were already being advanced by a substantial body of legal scholars as early as the late 19th century. It has also demonstrated that courts at both the state and federal levels were less formalist and more deferential to regulatory legislation during this period than is indicated by most historical accounts of the Lochner era. In particular, it has demonstrated that these accounts are at odds with the reality of a "legislative onslaught" of regulations enacted pursuant to states' police powers that began in the 1890s, "reached deep into the crevasses of social and economic life," and was only marginally affected by the invalidation of a comparatively small number of statutes.[89] Indeed, a number of early 20th century commentators even went as far as to praise the Supreme Court for its progressivism and its general friendliness toward regulatory legislation.[90] Such praise was generally premised upon the fact that the Supreme Court rejected more than three times as many substantive due process claims as it granted during the period between 1897 and 1937.[91] This illustrates that although the Court had a conservative majority and was on balance less progressive than Congress and most state legislatures during the 4th Party System, it embodied competing strains of jurisprudential thought that made its behavior less predictable than the conventional wisdom would indicate.

CONCLUSIONS

The dynamics underlying the relationship between the formalist turn in legal thought and the consolidation of the Republican political-electoral regime of the 4th Party System are distinct from the dynamics underlying the relationships between subsequent political-electoral regimes and their associated legal intellectual movements. While legal formalism, like legal realism and originalism, was a reflection of the political context in which it emerged, it was less dependent upon overt political support given the conservative politics of the elite ranks of the legal profession in the late 19th century and legal formalism's consistency with broader trends in the legal academy toward more abstract, integrated, and systematic concepts and classifications. Moreover, although legal formalism represented a new and distinctive approach to the law and its interpretation that departed significantly from 19th century legal thought, it differed from legal realism and originalism in that it did not arise as a challenge to the legal ideology of a decaying political-electoral regime. Instead, it represented an outgrowth of a bipartisan consensus that favored laissez faire economic policies and viewed organized labor and agrarian protest movements as grave threats to the social and political order. Furthermore, although the defenders of this consensus emerged victorious in the realigning election of 1896, they would increasingly be on the defensive in the years that followed as the Progressive Era unfolded. Indeed, despite the Bryan campaign's failure, many of its proposals for a more activist state would subsequently be embraced by the progressive movement, which succeeded in spearheading significant change at the national and state levels in the early 20th century. This success illustrated the coexistence of conservative and progressive factions within the Republican coalition, a coexistence that was reflected in a legal marketplace of idea that was far from monolithically formalist.

CHAPTER 5

Understanding the Relationship between Political and Legal Time

The results of this study show that the relationship between realignments of the political system and the rise of legal intellectual movements has not been constant over time but rather has been contingent upon the comprehensiveness of the realignment and upon how deeply entrenched the outgoing political-electoral regime's legal ideology is in the legal marketplace of ideas. In particular, a new legal intellectual movement that is affiliated with a regime that is the product of a partial and protracted realignment and which confronts a legal marketplace of ideas that remains thoroughly permeated by the outgoing regime's legal ideology will be highly reliant upon overt political support for legitimacy. This reliance is reflected in the close temporal relationship between the Reagan administration's campaign for a jurisprudence of original intention and the originalist turn in constitutional theory. Unlike other realignments of the political system, the realignment that gave rise to the New Right regime lacked a critical election giving Republicans control of both Congress and the presidency and unfolded over the course of several decades. This lack of a decisive reconstruction of the political order, coupled with the depth of legal liberalism's entrenchment in the organized bar, legal academy, and interest group system, resulted in originalists facing a relatively unfavorable environment for promoting their alternative constitutional vision. As Teles explains, legal liberalism, despite conservative trends in national politics, continued to be "strangely uncontroversial" in the legal profession and associated with "progress, modernity, and good professional practice."[1] Overcoming the liberal legal network's domination of the legal marketplace of ideas thus required the sort of external shock that only the Reagan administration's explicit embrace of originalism could provide.

Conversely, a new legal intellectual movement that is affiliated with a regime that is the product of a complete and rapid realignment and which confronts a legal marketplace of ideas that is less thoroughly permeated by the outgoing regime's legal ideology will be less reliant upon overt political support for legitimacy. This lack of reliance is reflected in the lack of a temporal relationship between the Roosevelt administration's various embraces of legal realism and the realist turn in legal thought. Unlike the partial and protracted realignment that gave rise to the New Right regime, the realignment that gave rise to the New Deal regime was both complete, culminating in the election of Democratic supermajorities in both houses of Congress and landslide Democratic victories in the 1932 and 1936 presidential elections, and rapid, precipitated by the sudden onset of the Great Depression in 1929 and largely completed by 1934. Not only did legal realists benefit from the fact that the New Deal earthquake realigned the political system much more thoroughly than did the conservative backlash that gave rise to the New Right regime, they also benefited from the fact that the legal ideology of their formalist opponents had never permeated the legal marketplace of ideas to the extent that legal liberalism later would. Although it continued to enjoy the strong support of the organized bar, formalism had long been a source of contention in the legal academy, having been the subject of prominent attacks by the proponents of sociological jurisprudence for nearly three decades. For these reasons, legal realism was able to flourish in the political and intellectual climate created by the Great Depression without the type of overt political support received by originalism.

The results of this study also show that the relationship between political realignment and change in the legal marketplace of ideas is contingent upon the ability of a new regime to articulate a legal ideology that unites its various constituencies. Unlike originalism, which united the New Right regime's ideologically disparate economic and social conservative constituencies, and legal realism, which united the New Deal regime's even more ideologically disparate collection of constituencies, legal formalism was a source of intense division for the 4th Party System's Republican regime. Although the conservative leadership of the Republican Party embraced legal formalism in the critical election of 1896, this appears to have had no effect upon legal discourse, a failure that may be attributed to the fact that many prominent figures associated with the party's progressive faction subsequently attacked legal formalism using rhetoric that echoed that of the party's Democratic opponents. Indeed, the data suggest that formalism was increasingly on the wane in the elite publications that set the tone for the legal marketplace of ideas after the election of 1896 (although it continued to be well represented in the rank and file of the legal profession). That the political triumph of the champions of legal formalism was contemporaneous with the beginning of legal formalism's decline as a legal intellectual movement indicates that the nature of partisan competition is an important determinant of the extent to which change in the legal marketplace of ideas is consistent with change in electoral politics. In particular, highly heterogeneous regimes constructed in periods in which interparty polarization is low and parties take relatively few monolithic positions are likely to be more constrained in their ability to successfully advance a legal ideology than homogeneous regimes constructed in periods in which interparty polarization is high.

The results also indicate the practical importance of changes in the climate of the legal marketplace of ideas insofar as these changes appear to have played an important role in allowing regimes to use judicial appointments to implement their constitutional visions. In particular, the rise in the law schools of the legal ideologies associated with these regimes corresponded in each case to the rise of new generations of lawyers who brought to the bench distinctive approaches to the law that reflected the influence of these legal ideologies. This pattern suggests that future Democratic control of the presidency would likely not move the Supreme Court in as liberal a direction as might be anticipated. Given that future nominees to the Court will be drawn from the ranks of lawyers whose legal education and professionalization occurred during the height of conservative trends in legal thought in the 1980s and 90s, a return to the liberal activism of the Warren and Burger Courts would be unlikely even if the partisan balance on the Court were to change significantly. Instead, future Democratic appointees will be increasingly likely to embody the centrism of Sonia Sotomayor and Elena Kagan. Conversely, it is likely that future Republican control of the presidency would move the Court in a more conservative direction as future Republican appointees will be lawyers in the mold of John Roberts and Samuel Alito, lawyers whose legal conservatism was forged in a more supportive environment than their forebears. Thus, just as "the life of the law has not been logic, it has been experience," to a significant extent the life of the Court has also not been logic but experience, the life experiences of its justices.[2]

The future development of the law will also depend upon the place of the Obama presidency in political time. In particular, it will depend upon whether Obama is merely a preemptive president in the New Right regime or a reconstructive president ushering in a new era of Democratic hegemony. The magnitude of Obama's victory in the election of 2008, the fact that it followed closely on the heels of the Democratic Party regaining majorities in both houses of Congress in 2006, and the fact that changing demographics continue to make the electorate more Democratic have led many to conclude that Obama is indeed a reconstructive president.[3] However, the Democratic Party's resounding defeats in the 2010 and 2014 midterm elections, the narrowness of Obama's reelection in 2012, and Obama's unwillingness to repudiate many of the policies of his Republican predecessor do not fit the pattern of reconstructive presidencies and have led others to conclude that Obama is a preemptive president.[4] While future elections will provide a more definitive answer to the question of Obama's place in political time, it is clear thus far that Obama has had less success in fundamentally changing the terms of political debates and vanquishing his political opponents than have previous reconstructive presidents.

Obama's status as a leader of legal change in the tradition of reconstructive presidents such as Franklin Roosevelt and Ronald Reagan is similarly ambiguous. On the one hand, Obama has been quite vocal in criticizing the Roberts Court at times, most notably using his 2010 State of the Union address to lambaste the Court's decision in *Citizens United v. Federal Election Commission*. This has drawn comparisons to the anti-judicial rhetoric of Roosevelt and Reagan.[5] Obama has also occasionally engaged in the sort of departmentalist rhetoric that has been typical of reconstructive presidents, preemptively attacking "judicial activism" and the prospect that "an unelected group of people would somehow overturn a duly constituted and passed law" when confronted with the possibility of the Supreme Court declaring the Patient Protection and Affordable Care Act unconstitutional.[6] Obama's statements that his Supreme Court nominees would be jurists in the mold of Earl Warren who possessed "empathy" and identified "with people's hopes and struggles" also led many to believe that he would pursue a transformative legal agenda that would challenge formalist trends in legal thought and jurisprudence.[7] However, on the other hand, Obama's actual record of judicial appointments has drawn comparisons to those of other preemptive presidents insofar as it has been widely described as "narrow and unadventurous" in its avoidance of controversy and potential failure by choosing moderate liberals over more transformative alternatives.[8]

If Obama's place in legal time is also best understood as that of a preemptive president, his impact on the Court and on the legal marketplace of ideas will depend upon which issues he chooses to preempt and which issues he chooses to contest. The fact that he has chosen to contest relatively few indicates that this impact is likely to be rather limited. With the exception of Obama's half-hearted attempt to limit the impact of the Court's decision in *Citizens United* by issuing a vague call for new campaign finance legislation, his administration has done little to act against the Roberts Court. This is perhaps not surprising given that the Court has continued to affirm *Roe v. Wade* and has generally delivered few decisions that conflict with the administration's other core priorities. This is due in large part to the fact that these priorities have been defined relatively narrowly. Although landmark decisions such as *District of Columbia v. Heller*, in which the Court declared that the 2nd Amendment protects an individual right to possess a firearm, have been denounced by many liberals, Barack Obama has not been among them.

Moreover, even if the Obama administration were committed to more fundamental legal change, it would find that a president's ability to effect such change through Supreme Court appointments has declined due to the changing institutional dynamics of the Court. As Crowe and Karpowitz illustrate, the average length of tenure of a Supreme Court justice has increased significantly since the 1970s.[9] This has made vacancies on the Court less frequent and has made it more difficult for presidents and regimes to remake the Court in their image. For example, if all five of the Republican appointees currently on the Court serve until they are as old as the most recent justice to leave the Court, John Paul Stevens, was when he retired, Democrats would need to wait until 2026 for the opportunity to give the Court a Democratic majority. This is emblematic of what Skowronek has termed the "waning of political time," the waning ability of presidents to transform the political order due to "institutional thickening."[10] While Skowronek uses this term primarily to describe the accrual of power within the executive branch by the bureaucracy, it is also an apt description of the Supreme Court's increasing insulation from the cycle of political time.

This insulation has arguably made the efforts of regimes to promote their legal ideologies in the legal marketplace of ideas more consequential insofar as these efforts are now likely to leave longer legacies that will outlive those regimes to a greater degree than they would have in the past. This study indicates that these efforts succeed through a process of issue evolution in the legal marketplace of ideas that is analogous to the process of issue evolution in mass publics. Just as change in the partisan balance in the electorate is driven by signals from political actors indicating changes in issue alignments, change in the ideological balance in the legal marketplace of ideas can be driven by signals from political actors indicating their alignment with a legal ideology. In particular, just as political issues lay dormant for long periods of time prior to political elites giving them partisan valence that realigns the electorate, originalism had lain politically dormant in the legal academy prior to suddenly acquiring partisan valence as a result of the Reagan administration's campaign for a jurisprudence of original intention. To a somewhat lesser extent, the same can be said of legal realism, as anti-formalism had faded as a rallying cry for Democrats prior to the campaign led by Democrats in the Senate to defeat the Parker nomination. Moreover, it appears that the acquisition of partisan valence by these legal ideologies played a major role in realigning the legal marketplace of ideas in a manner that, consistent with trends in national politics, saw these legal ideologies increasingly come to define mainstream legal thought. Thus, just as most policy debates engaged in by political elites generally attract little public notice unless they are framed as partisan issues by political actors who have an interest in doing so, most legal and constitutional debates are similarly autonomous unless they are framed as partisan debates by political actors who have an interest in seeing them become powerful drivers of legal change.

Finally, the role of political actors in directing the development of legal theory also suggests the limitations of progressive theories of law that view litigation as a key instrument for the achievement of social reform. In particular, this study's findings underscore the validity of one of the major concerns expressed by critics of these theories, which is that courts lack sufficient independence from the political branches of government to act as independent agents of social reform.[11] As the prism through which the law is interpreted is likely to reflect the interests and preferences of the dominant national political coalition, the ability of courts to move the law in directions inconsistent with these interests and preferences is limited. While this may be a source of disappointment for activists who seek to use the courts to achieve social change, it is likely to be a source of encouragement for those concerned about the democratic legitimacy of judicial review. Most importantly, the results of this study suggest that to truly understand the relationship between politics and jurisprudence, it is necessary to look beyond the traditional focus on judicial appointments and to the deeper ways in which political change structures ways of thinking about the law.

Notes

CHAPTER 1

1. Steven Teles, *The Rise of the Conservative Legal Movement: The Battle for Control of the Law* (Princeton: Princeton University Press, 2008), 166.
2. Robert Dahl, "Decision-Making in a Democracy: The Supreme Court as National Policy-Maker," *Journal of Public Law* 6 (1957): 279-95, 293.
3. Alexander Bickel, *The Least Dangerous Branch: The Supreme Court at the Bar of Politics* (New Haven: Yale University Press, 1962), 18, 16.
4. *See e.g.* Sheldon Goldman, *Picking Federal Judges: Lower Court Selection from Roosevelt through Reagan* (New Haven: Yale University Press, 1999); Lee Epstein and Jeffrey Segal, *Advice and Consent: The Politics of Judicial Appointments* (Oxford: Oxford University Press, 2005); Sarah Binder and Forrest Maltzman, *Advice and Dissent: The Struggle to Shape the Federal Judiciary* (Washington: The Brookings Institution, 2009).
5. Stephen Skowronek, *The Politics Presidents Make: Leadership from John Adams to Bill Clinton* (Cambridge, MA: Harvard University Press, 1993).
6. Ibid., 41.
7. Keith Whittington, *Political Foundations of Judicial Supremacy: The Presidency, the Supreme Court, and Constitutional Leadership in U.S. History* (Princeton: Princeton University Press, 2007), 77.
8. Cornell Clayton and J. Mitchell Pickerill, "The Politics of Criminal Justice: How the New Right Regime Shaped the Rehnquist Court's Criminal Justice Jurisprudence," *Georgetown Law Journal* 94 (2006): 1385-1425.
9. Cornell Clayton and J. Mitchell Pickerill, "The Rehnquist Court and the Political Dynamics of Federalism," *Perspectives on Politics* 2 (2004): 233-48; Cornell Clayton and J. Mitchell Pickerill, "Guess What Happened on the Way to Revolution? Precursors to the Supreme Court's Federalism Revolution," *Publius* 34 (2004): 85-114.
10. Thomas Keck, *The Most Activist Supreme Court in History: The Road to Modern Judicial Conservatism* (Chicago: University of Chicago Press, 2004), 13.
11. Ibid., 156.
12. Ibid., 185.
13. *See* Keith Whittington, "'Interpose Your Friendly Hand:' Political Supports for the Exercise of Judicial Review by the United States Supreme Court,"

American Political Science Review 99 (2005): 583-96; Whittington, *Political Foundations of Judicial Supremacy*.

14. Whittington, *Political Foundations of Judicial Supremacy*, 86.
15. *See* Mark Graber, "The Non-Majoritarian Difficulty: Legislative Deference to the Judiciary," *Studies in American Political Development* 7 (1993): 35 73; George Lovell, *Legislative Deferrals: Statutory Ambiguity, Judicial Power, and American Democracy* (Cambridge: Cambridge University Press, 2003).
16. Graber, "The Non-Majoritarian Difficulty," 46.
17. Ibid., 48.
18. Howard Gillman, "How Parties Can Use the Courts to Advance Their Agendas: Federal Courts in the United States, 1875-1891," *American Political Science Review* 96 (2002): 511-24, 514.
19. Ran Hirschl, *Towards Juristocracy: The Origins and Consequences of the New Constitutionalism* (Cambridge, MA: Harvard University Press, 2004), 43.
20. Edward Carmines and James Stimson, "Issue Evolution, Population Replacement, and Normal Partisan Change," *American Political Science Review* 75 (1981): 107-18; Edward Carmines and James Stimson, "On the Structure and Sequence of Issue Evolution," *American Political Science Review* 80 (1986): 901-20.
21. Karen Orren and Stephen Skowronek, *The Search for American Political Development* (Cambridge: Cambridge University Press, 2004), 108.
22. Gary Miller and Norman Schofield, "The Transformation of the Republican and Democratic Party Coalitions in the U.S.," *Perspectives on Politics* 6 (2008): 433-50, 439.
23. Orren and Skowronek, *The Search for American Political Development*, 17.
24. *See* Charles Epp, *The Rights Revolution: Lawyers, Activists, and Supreme Courts in Comparative Perspective* (Chicago: University of Chicago Press, 1998); Teles, *The Rise of the Conservative Legal Movement*.
25. Epp, *The Rights Revolution*, 200.
26. Ibid., 199.
27. Teles, *The Rise of the Conservative Legal Movement*, 12.
28. *See for example* Grant Gilmore, *The Ages of American Law* (New Haven: Yale University Press, 1977); Kermit Hall, *The Magic Mirror: Law in American History* (Oxford: Oxford University Press, 1989); Neil Duxbury, *Patterns of American Jurisprudence* (Oxford: Oxford University Press, 1995).
29. Teles, *The Rise of the Conservative Legal Movement*, 28.

30. Ibid., 29.
31. James Sundquist, *Dynamics of the Party System: Alignment and Realignment of Political Parties in the United States* (Washington: The Brookings Institution, 1983), 155.
32. *See e.g.* Walter Dean Burnham, *Critical Elections and the Mainsprings of American Politics* (New York: W.W. Norton & Company, 1971); Walter Dean Burnham, "Periodization Schemes and 'Party Systems:' The System of 1896 as a Case in Point," *Social Science History* 10 (1986): 263-314; John Gerring, *Party Ideologies in America, 1828-1996* (Cambridge: Cambridge University Press, 1998).
33. *See e.g.* Daniel Boorstin, *The Americans: The National Experience* (New York: Vintage Books, 1967); Morton Horwitz, *The Transformation of American Law, 1780-1860* (Oxford: Oxford University Press, 1992); William Novak, *The People's Welfare: Law and Regulation in 19th Century America* (Chapel Hill: University of North Carolina Press, 1996).
34. *See e.g.* Gilmore, *The Ages of American Law*; Morton Horwitz, *The Transformation of American Law 1870-1960: The Crisis of Legal Orthodoxy* (Oxford: Oxford University Press, 1992); William Wiecek, *The Lost World of Classical Legal Thought: Law and Ideology in America, 1886-1937* (Oxford: Oxford University Press, 1998).
35. *See e.g.* Horwitz, *The Transformation of American Law, 1780-1860*; Horwitz, *The Transformation of American Law 1870-1960*; Wiecek, *The Lost World of Classical Legal Thought.*
36. *See e.g.* Alan Furman Westin, "The Supreme Court, the Populist Movement, and the Campaign of 1896," *Journal of Politics* 15 (1953): 3-41; Sundquist, *Dynamics of the Party System*; Gerring, *Party Ideologies in America, 1828-1996.*
37. *See e.g.* Laura Kalman, *Legal Realism at Yale, 1927-1960* (Chapel Hill: University of North Carolina Press, 1986); Joseph Singer, "Legal Realism Now," *California Law Review* 76 (1988): 468-544; Horwitz, *The Transformation of American Law 1870-1960.*
38. *See* Ken Kersch, *Constructing Civil Liberties: Discontinuities in the Development of American Constitutional Law* (Cambridge: Cambridge University Press, 2004).
39. *See e.g.* Melvin Urofsky, "Conflict among the Brethren: Felix Frankfurter, William O. Douglas, and the Clash of Personalities and Philosophies on the United States Supreme Court," *Duke Law Journal* 1988 (1988): 71-113; Thomas Keck, "Activism and Restraint on the Rehnquist Court: Timing,

Sequence, and Conjuncture in Constitutional Development," *Polity* 35 (2002): 121-52; Keck, *The Most Activist Supreme Court in History*.

40. *See for example* Martha Derthick and Paul Quirk, *The Politics of Deregulation* (Washington: The Brookings Institution, 1985); David Garland, *The Culture of Control: Crime and Social Order in Contemporary Society* (Chicago: University of Chicago Press, 2001); Brian Domitrovic, *Econoclasts: The Rebels Who Sparked the Supply-Side Revolution and Restored American Prosperity* (Wilmington, DE: Intercollegiate Studies Institute, 2009).
41. *See e.g.* Johnathan O'Neill, "Shaping Modern Constitutional Theory: Bickel and Bork Confront the Warren Court," *Review of Politics* 65 (2003): 325-51; Johnathan O'Neill, *Originalism in American Law and Politics: A Constitutional_History* (Baltimore: Johns Hopkins University Press, 2005); Steven Calabresi, *Originalism: A Quarter-Century of Debate* (Washington: Regnery Publishing, 2007).
42. James Fleming, "The Balkanization of Originalism," *Maryland Law Review* 67 (2007): 10-13, 10.
43. *See for example* O'Neill, *Originalism in American Law and Politics*; Joan Biskupic, *American Original: The Life and Constitution of Supreme Court Justice Antonin Scalia* (New York: Farrar, Straus & Giroux, 2009); Jeffrey Toobin, *The Oath: The Obama White House and the Supreme Court* (New York: Doubleday, 2012).
44. *See for example* Paul Gottfried and Thomas Fleming, *The Conservative Movement* (New York: Twayne Publishers, 1988), 65; George Nash, *The Conservative Intellectual Movement in America since 1945* (Wilmington, DE: Intercollegiate Studies Institute, 1998), 101; Ann Southworth, *Lawyers of the Right: Professionalizing the Conservative Coalition* (Chicago: University of Chicago Press, 2008), 107-8.
45. *See e.g.* G. Edward White, "From Sociological Jurisprudence to Realism: Jurisprudence and Social Change in Early Twentieth Century America," *Virginia Law Review* 58 (1972): 999-1028; Hall, *The Magic Mirror*; Horwitz, *The Transformation of American Law 1870-1960*.
46. *See* Owen Fiss, "Objectivity and Interpretation," *Stanford Law Review* 34 (1982): 739-63; Jack Balkin, "Bush v. Gore and the Boundary between Law and Politics," *Yale Law Journal* 110 (2001): 1407-58.
47. Jack Balkin and Sanford Levinson, "Understanding the Constitutional Revolution," *Virginia Law Review* 87 (2001): 1045-1104, 1092.
48. Teles, *The Rise of the Conservative Legal Movement*, 42.

49. *See* Fred Shapiro, "The Most Cited Law Reviews," *Journal of Legal Studies* 29 (2000): 389-96; Ronen Perry, "The Relative Value of American Law Reviews: A Critical Appraisal of Ranking Methods," *Connecticut Law Review* 39 (2006): 1-41.
50. Bernard Hibbitts, "Last Writes? Reassessing the Law Review in the Age of Cyberspace," *New York University Law Review* 71 (1996): 615-88.
51. Herbert Wechsler, "Toward Neutral Principles of Constitutional Law," *Harvard Law Review* 73 (1959): 1-35; Robert Bork, "Neutral Principles and Some First Amendment Problems," *Indiana Law Journal* 47 (1971): 1-35; Raoul Berger, *Government by Judiciary: The Transformation of the 14th Amendment* (Cambridge, MA: Harvard University Press, 1977).
52. Horwitz, *The Transformation of American Law 1870-1960*, 187.
53. White, "From Sociological Jurisprudence to Realism," 999.
54. *See e.g.* Peter Irons, *The New Deal Lawyers* (Princeton: Princeton University Press, 1982); Michael Belknap, "The New Deal and the Emergency Powers Doctrine," *Texas Law Review* 62 (1983): 67-109; Daniel Hulsebosch, "The New Deal Court: Emergence of a New Reason," *Columbia Law Review* 90 (1990): 1973-2016.
55. *See e.g.* Gilmore, *The Ages of American Law*; Horwitz, *The Transformation of American Law 1870-1960*; Wiecek, *The Lost World of Classical Legal Thought*.
56. Howard Gillman, *The Constitution Besieged: The Rise and Demise of Lochner Era Police Powers Jurisprudence* (Durham, NC: Duke University Press, 1993), 8.
57. Morton Horwitz, "The Rise of Legal Formalism," *American Journal of Legal History* 19 (1975): 251-64.
58. *See e.g.* Gilmore, *The Ages of American Law*; Horwitz, *The Transformation of American Law 1870-1960*; Wiecek, *The Lost World of Classical Legal Thought*.
59. *See e.g.* Kalman, *Legal Realism at Yale, 1927-1960*; Singer, "Legal Realism Now," Horwitz, *The Transformation of American Law 1870-1960.*
60. Kersch, *Constructing Civil Liberties*, 17-25.
61. Southworth, *Lawyers of the Right*, 107.
62. *See e.g.* Bork, "Neutral Principles and Some First Amendment Problems;" Berger, *Government by Judiciary*; Antonin Scalia, "Originalism: The Lesser Evil," *University of Cincinnati Law Review* 57 (1989): 849-64.
63. Southworth, *Lawyers of the Right*, 107.
64. John Schmidhauser, *Constitutional Law in American Politics* (Monterey, CA: Brooks/Cole Publishing Company, 1984); Andrew Martin and Kevin

Quinn, "Dynamic Ideal Point Estimation via Markov Chain Monte Carlo for the U.S. Supreme Court, 1953-1999," *Political Analysis* 10 (2002): 134-53.

65. *See e.g.* Ronald Dworkin, *Taking Rights Seriously* (Cambridge, MA: Harvard University Press, 1977); Bruce Ackerman, *Social Justice in the Liberal State* (New Haven: Yale University Press, 1980); Michael McCann, *Rights at Work: Pay Equity Reform and the Politics of Legal Mobilization* (Chicago: University of Chicago Press, 1994).

CHAPTER 2

1. Fleming, "The Balkanization of Originalism," 10.
2. Ibid.
3. Stephen Carter, "Bork Redux, or How the Tempting of America Led the People to Rise and Battle for Justice," *Texas Law Review* 69 (1991): 759-93, 783.
4. *See e.g.* Jonathan Knuckey, "Classification of Presidential Elections: An Update," *Polity* 31 (1999): 639-53; James Campbell, "Party Systems and Realignments in the United States, 1868-2004," *Social Science History* 30 (2006): 359-86; Rick Perlstein, *Nixonland: The Rise of a President and the Fracturing of America* (New York: Simon & Schuster, 2008).
5. *See e.g.* Sundquist, *Dynamics of the Party System*; Michael MacKuen, Robert Erikson, and James Stimson, "Macropartisanship," *American Political Science Review* 83 (1989): 1125-42; Donald Green, Bradley Palmquist, and Eric Schickler, *Partisan Hearts and Minds: Parties and the Social Identities of Voters* (New Haven: Yale University Press, 2002).
6. *See e.g.* Martin Wattenberg, *The Decline of American Political Parties, 1952-1996* (Cambridge, MA: Harvard University Press, 1998); Steven Rosenstone and John Mark Hansen, *Mobilization, Participation, and Democracy in America* (New York: Longman, 2002); Morris Fiorina, *Divided Government* (New York: Longman, 2003).
7. Sundquist, *Dynamics of the Party System*, 383.
8. Kevin Phillips, *The Emerging Republican Majority* (New York: Anchor Books, 1969).
9. Sundquist, *Dynamics of the Party System*, 393.
10. *See e.g.* Andrew Busch, *Reagan's Victory: The Presidential Election of 1980 and the Rise of the Right* (Lawrence: University Press of Kansas, 2005); Gil Troy, *Morning in America: How Ronald Reagan Invented the 1980s* (Princeton: Princeton University Press, 2005); Craig Shirley,

Rendezvous with Destiny: Ronald Reagan and the Campaign That Changed America (Wilmington, DE: Intercollegiate Studies Institute, 2009).

11. *See e.g.* Jeff Smith, "Trading Places: The Two Parties in the Electorate from 1975-2004" (Ph.D. dissertation, Washington University in St. Louis, 2005); Norman Schofield and Gary Miller, "Elections and Activist Coalitions in the United States," *American Journal of Political Science* 51 (2007): 518-31; Miller and Schofield, "The Transformation of the Republican and Democratic Party Coalitions in the U.S."
12. *See e.g.* Steven Shier, ed., *The Post-Modern Presidency: Bill Clinton's Legacy in U.S. Politics* (Pittsburgh: University of Pittsburgh Press, 2000); Daniel Béland and Alex Waddan, "The Social Policies Presidents Make: Preemptive Leadership under Nixon and Clinton," *Political Studies* 54 (2006): 65-83; Zachary Mancher, "The Presidents Skowronek Forgot: How Preemptive Presidents Follow Similar Paths in Campaigns, Domestic Policy, and Foreign Policy As Shown Through Eisenhower and Clinton," *Colgate Academic Review* 5 (2009): 84-92.
13. *See e.g.* Earl Black and Merle Black, *Politics and Society in the South* (Cambridge, MA: Harvard University Press, 1989); Alexander Lamis, ed., *Southern Politics in the 1990s* (Baton Rouge: Louisiana State University Press, 1999); Earl Black and Merle Black, *The Rise of Southern Republicans* (Cambridge, MA: Belknap Press, 2002).
14. Nolan McCarty, Keith Poole, and Howard Rosenthal, *Polarized America: The Dance of Ideology and Unequal Riches* (Cambridge, MA: M.I.T. Press, 2008), 15-70.
15. O'Neill, *Originalism in American Law and Politics*, 12-42.
16. Teles, *The Rise of the Conservative Legal Movement*, 22-57.
17. Ibid., 28.
18. Laura Kalman, *The Strange Career of Legal Liberalism* (New Haven: Yale University Press, 1996), 52.
19. Ibid.
20. Teles, *The Rise of the Conservative Legal Movement*, 42.
21. Ibid.
22. Ibid., 45.
23. Martin Shapiro, "Interest Groups and Supreme Court Appointments," *Northwestern Law Review* 84 (1990): 935-61, 955.
24. Heather MacDonald, "This is the Legal Mainstream?" *City Journal* 16 (2006): Accessed November 22, 2014, http://www.city-journal.org/html/16_1_law_schools.html.

25. Walter Olson, *Schools for Misrule: Legal Academia and an Overlawyered America* (New York: Encounter Books, 2011), 103.
26. Teles, *The Rise of the Conservative Legal Movement*, 46-51.
27. Olson, *Schools for Misrule*, 98.
28. Ibid., 97.
29. Teles, *The Rise of the Conservative Legal Movement*, 48.
30. Ibid., 23.
31. Ibid., 48.
32. Olson, *Schools for Misrule*, 98.
33. Teles, *The Rise of the Conservative Legal Movement*, 139-40.
34. Ibid., 135-80.
35. *See e.g.* John Heinz, Ann Southworth, and Anthony Paik, "Lawyers for Conservative Causes: Clients, Ideology, and Social Distance," *Law & Society Review* 37 (2003): 5-50; Southworth, *Lawyers of the Right*; Nancy Scherer and Banks Miller, "The Federalist Society's Influence on the Federal Judiciary," *Political Research Quarterly* 62 (2009): 366-78.
36. Teles, *The Rise of the Conservative Legal Movement*, 220-64.
37. *See e.g.* James McGann, "Academics to Ideologues: A Brief History of the Public Policy Research Industry," *PS: Political Science & Politics* 25 (1992): 733-740; Ken Kersch, "Ecumenicalism Through Constitutionalism: The Discursive Development of Constitutional Conservatism in National Review, 1955-1980," *Studies in American Political Development* 25 (2011): 86-116; Lee Edwards, *Leading the Way: The Story of Ed Feulner and the Heritage Foundation* (New York: Crown Forum, 2013).
38. *See* Daniel Lowenstein, Review of *The Rise of the Conservative Legal Movement: The Battle for Control of the Law* by Stephen Teles, *Engage* 9 (2008): 116-18.
39. *See* Olson, *Schools for Misrule*, 14-17.
40. Lowenstein, Review of *The Rise of the Conservative Legal Movement*, 118.
41. Cass Sunstein, "On Academic Fads and Fashions," *Michigan Law Review* 99 (2001): 1251-64, 1262.
42. David Barnhizer, "Prophets, Priests, and Power Blockers: Three Fundamental Roles of Judges and Legal Scholars in America," *University of Pittsburgh Law Review* 50 (1988): 127-96, 151.
43. Ibid.
44. Balkin, "Bush v. Gore and the Boundary between Law and Politics," 1444.
45. *See e.g.* Lewis Chester, Godfrey Hodgson, and Bruce Page, *An American Melodrama: The Presidential Campaign of 1968* (New York: Viking Press,

1969); Thomas Edsall and Mary Edsall, *Chain Reaction: The Impact of Race, Rights, and Taxes on American Politics* (New York: W.W. Norton & Company, 1991); Clayton and Pickerill, "The Politics of Criminal Justice."

46. *See e.g.* William Rehnquist, "The Notion of a Living Constitution." *Texas Law Review* 54 (1976): 693-706; Sue Davis, *Justice Rehnquist and the Constitution* (Princeton: Princeton University Press, 1989); O'Neill, *Originalism in American Law and Politics*, 160.
47. *See e.g.* Jerold Israel, "Criminal Procedure, the Burger Court, and the Legacy of the Warren Court," *Michigan Law Review* 75 (1977): 1319-1425; Carol Steiker, "Counter-Revolution in Constitutional Criminal Procedure? Two Audiences, Two Answers," *Michigan Law Review* 94 (1996): 2466-2551; Clayton and Pickerill, "The Politics of Criminal Justice."
48. *See* Kevin McMahon, *Nixon's Court: His Challenge to Judicial Liberalism and Its Political Consequences* (Chicago: University of Chicago Press, 2011).
49. *See for example* Lucas McMillan and Cornell Clayton, "Context is Everything: The Roberts Court in a Polarized Political Regime" (Paper presented at the annual meeting of the American Political Science Association, New Orleans, LA, August 30-September 2, 2012).
50. Vincent Blasi, *The Burger Court: The Counter-Revolution That Wasn't* (New Haven: Yale University Press, 1986).
51. O'Neill, *Originalism in American Law and Politics*, 146.
52. Teles, *The Rise of the Conservative Legal Movement*, 13.
53. Ibid., 137-42.
54. Edward Lazarus, *Closed Chambers: The First Eyewitness Account of the Epic Struggles inside the Supreme Court* (New York: Random House, 1998), 264.
55. O'Neill, *Originalism in American Law and Politics*, 148.
56. Teles, *The Rise of the Conservative Legal Movement*, 145.
57. Kersch, "Ecumenicalism Through Constitutionalism," 87.
58. Robert Post and Reva Siegel, "Originalism as a Political Practice: The Right's Living Constitution," *Fordham Law Review* 75 (2006): 545-574, 570.
59. Jack Rakove, *Original Meanings: Politics and Ideas in the Making of the Constitution* (New York: Vintage Books, 1997), 22.
60. Cornell Clayton, *The Politics of Justice: The Attorney General and the Making of Legal Policy* (New York: M.E. Sharpe, Inc., 1992), 150.
61. Steven Calabresi, *Originalism: A Quarter-Century of Debate* (Washington: Regnery Publishing, 2007), 52.

62. Ibid., 54.
63. W. Wat Hopkins, *Mr. Justice Brennan and Freedom of Expression* (Westport, CT: Greenwood Press, 1991), 2.
64. O'Neill, *Originalism in American Law and Politics*, 157.
65. *See for example* Edwin Meese, "The Supreme Court of the United States: Bulwark of a Limited Constitution," *South Texas Law Review* 27 (1986): 455-66; Edwin Meese, "Our Constitution's Design: Implications for Its Interpretation," *Marquette Law Review* 70 (1987): 380-88; Edwin Meese, "Constitutional Fidelity and Foreign Affairs," *University of Miami Law Review* 43 (1988): 223-31.
66. Meese, "Our Constitution's Design," 388.
67. United States Department of Justice Office of Legal Policy, *Original Meaning Jurisprudence: A Sourcebook* (Washington: United States Department of Justice, 1987); United States Department of Justice Office of Legal Policy, *The Constitution in the Year 2000: Choices Ahead in Constitutional Interpretation* (Washington: United States Department of Justice, 1988).
68. United States Department of Justice Office of Legal Policy, *Original Meaning Jurisprudence*, 4, 23.
69. Steven Teles, "Transformative Bureaucracy: Reagan's Lawyers and the Dynamics of Political Investment," *Studies in American Political Development* 23 (2009): 61-83.
70. Morton Horwitz, "The Meaning of the Bork Nomination in American Constitutional History," *University of Pittsburgh Law Review* 50 (1989): 655-64, 655.
71. Paul Dimond, "Common Sense about an Uncommon Rejection," *Law & Social Inquiry* 15 (1990): 767-804, 769.
72. Gregory Caldeira, Marie Hojnacki, and John Wright, "The Lobbying Activities of Organized Interests in Federal Judicial Nominations," *Journal of Politics* 62 (2000): 51-69, 57.
73. John Broder, "Edward Kennedy, Senate Stalwart, Dies," *New York Times*, August 26, 2009.
74. Bruce Ackerman, "Transformative Appointments," *Harvard Law Review* 101 (1988): 1164-84, 1178.
75. Robert Nagel, "Meeting the Enemy," *University of Chicago Law Review* 57 (1990): 633-56, 633.
76. O'Neill, *Originalism in American Law and Politics*, 186.
77. Ronald Collins and David Skover, "The Future of Liberal Legal Scholarship," *Michigan Law Review* 87 (1988): 189-239, 201.

78. *See e.g.* Richard Brisbin, *Justice Antonin Scalia and the Conservative Revival* (Baltimore: Johns Hopkins University Press, 1998); Ralph Rossum, *Antonin Scalia's Jurisprudence: Text and Tradition* (Lawrence: University Press of Kansas, 2006); Joan Biskupic, *American Original: The Life and Constitution of Supreme Court Justice Antonin Scalia* (New York: Farrar, Straus & Giroux, 2009).
79. Collins and Skover, "The Future of Liberal Legal Scholarship," 200.
80. O'Neill, *Originalism in American Law and Politics*, 161.
81. *See e.g.* Frank Guliuzza, Daniel Reagan, and David Barrett, "The Senate Judiciary Committee and Supreme Court Nominees: Measuring the Dynamics of Confirmation Criteria," *Journal of Politics* 56 (1994): 773-87; Ayo Ogundele and Linda Camp Keith, "Reexamining the Impact of the Bork Nomination to the Supreme Court," *Political Research Quarterly* 52 (1999): 403-20; Lori Ringhand and Paul Collins, "May It Please the Senate: An Empirical Analysis of the Senate Judiciary Committee Hearings of Supreme Court Nominees, 1939-2009," *American University Law Review* 60 (2011): 589-641.
82.Michael McConnell, "The Origins and Historical Understanding of Free Exercise of Religion," *Harvard Law Review* 103 (1990): 1409-1517, 1409; Richard Epstein, "Toward a Revitalization of the Contract Clause," *University of Chicago Law Review* 51 (1984): 703-51, 710.
83. Douglas Kmiec, "The Original Understanding of the Taking Clause Is Neither Weak nor Obtuse," *Columbia Law Review* 88 (1988): 1630-66, 1666; Eric Schnapper, "Affirmative Action and the Legislative History of the 14th Amendment," *Virginia Law Review* 71 (1985): 753-98, 754.
84. Lino Graglia, "'Constitutional Theory:' The Attempted Justification for the Supreme Court's Liberal Political Program," *Texas Law Review* 65 (1987): 789-98, 798, 792.
85. Erwin Chemerinsky, "Empty History," *Michigan Law Review* 81 (1983): 828-38, 834.
86. H. Jefferson Powell, "The Original Understanding of Original Intent," *Harvard Law Review* 98 (1985): 885-948, 885.
87. Louis Seidman, "Public Principle and Private Choice: The Uneasy Case for a Boundary Maintenance Theory of Constitutional Law," *Yale Law Journal* 96 (1987): 1006-59, 1049.
88. Teles, *The Rise of the Conservative Legal Movement*, 149.
89. Ibid., 150.
90. Ibid.
91. Clayton, *The Politics of Justice*, 71.

92. "A Radical Intent," *Harvard Law Review* 101 (1988): 869-73, 872.
93. Michael Curtis, *No State Shall Abridge: The 14th Amendment and the Bill of Rights* (Durham, NC: Duke University Press, 1986).
94. Ibid., 10.
95. Nina Morais, "Sex Discrimination and the 14th Amendment: Lost History," *Yale Law Journal* 97 (1988): 1153-72.
96. Ibid., 1172.
97. Schnapper, "Affirmative Action and the Legislative History of the 14th Amendment;" Lea Vander Velde, "The Labor Vision of the 13th Amendment," *University of Pennsylvania Law Review* 138 (1989): 437-504; *See also e.g.* Robert Kaczorowski, "Revolutionary Constitutionalism in the Era of the Civil War and Reconstruction," *New York University Law Review* 61 (1986): 863-940; Julius Chambers, "Protection of Civil Rights: A Constitutional Mandate for the Federal Government," *Michigan Law Review* 87 (1989): 1599-1614; Douglas Colbert, "Challenging the Challenge: The 13th Amendment as a Prohibition Against the Racial Use of Preemptory Challenges," *Cornell Law Review* 76 (1990): 1-128.
98. O'Neill, *Originalism in American Law and Politics*, 131.
99. Berger, *Government by Judiciary*, xvii.
100. Raoul Berger, *Executive Privilege: A Constitutional Myth* (Cambridge, MA: Harvard University Press, 1974).
101. Raoul Berger, *Congress v. The Supreme Court* (Cambridge, MA: Harvard University Press, 1969).
102. Randall Bridwell, Review of *Government by Judiciary: The Transformation of the 14th Amendment* by Raoul Berger, *Duke Law Journal* 1978 (1978): 907-20, 908; Michael Perry, Review of *Government by Judiciary: The Transformation of the 14th Amendment* by Raoul Berger, *Columbia Law Review* 78 (1978): 685-705, 691.
103. Walter Murphy, "Constitutional Interpretation: The Art of the Historian, Magician, or Statesman?" *Yale Law Journal* 87 (1978): 1752-71, 1761.
104. Jack Balkin, "Constitutional Interpretation and the Problem of History," *New York University Law Review* 63 (1988): 911-54; H. Jefferson Powell, "The Modern Misunderstanding of Original Intent," *University of Chicago Law Review* 54 (1987): 1513-44.
105. Michael McConnell, "Federalism: Evaluating the Founders' Design," *University of Chicago Law Review* 54 (1987): 1484-1512, 1484; "Original Federalism," *Harvard Law Review* 101 (1988): 855-59, 859.
106. Robert Bork, *The Tempting of America: The Political Seduction of the Law* (New York: Macmillan Publishers, 1990).

107. Carter, "Bork Redux," 789, 783.
108. Lyle Denniston, "Mr. Bork Inquires into the Origin and Nature of Permissiveness," *Michigan Law Review* 88 (1990): 1291-99, 1294, 1293, 1294.
109. *See e.g.* Sanford Levinson, *Constitutional Faith* (Princeton: Princeton University Press, 1988); Keck, *The Most Activist Supreme Court in History*; Mark Graber, "Popular Constitutionalism, Judicial Supremacy, and the Complete Lincoln-Douglas Debates," *Chicago-Kent Law Review* 81 (2006): 923-51.
110. Teles, *The Rise of the Conservative Legal Movement*, 16.
111. Ibid., 23, 16.
112. Graber, "Popular Constitutionalism, Judicial Supremacy, and the Complete Lincoln-Douglas Debates," 943-44; Keck, *The Most Activist Supreme Court in History*, 278.
113. Mark Graber, "Does It Really Matter? Conservative Courts in a Conservative Era," *Fordham Law Review* 75 (2006): 675-708, 693.
114. Ibid., 706.
115. *See for example* J. Mitchell Pickerill, "Something Old, Something New, Something Borrowed, Something Blue," *Santa Clara Law Review* 49 (2009): 1063-1101.
116. Ken Foskett, *Judging Thomas: The Life and Times of Clarence Thomas* (New York: Harper Collins Publishers, 2004), 281.
117. Adam Liptak, "Justice Defends Ruling on Finance," *New York Times*, February 23, 2010; Foskett, *Judging Thomas*, 282.
118. *Dickerson v. United States*, 530 U.S. 428, 443 (2000).
119. Graber, "Popular Constitutionalism, Judicial Supremacy, and the Complete Lincoln-Douglas Debates," 944.
120. *See e.g.* Urofsky, "Conflict among the Brethren;" Barry Friedman, "The Birth of an Academic Obsession: The History of the Countermajoritarian Difficulty, Part Five," *Yale Law Journal* 112 (2002): 153-259; Keck, "Activism and Restraint on the Rehnquist Court."
121. David Kaplan, "The Reagan Court—Child of Lyndon Johnson?" *New York Times*, September 4, 1989.
122. Pickerill, "Something Old, Something New, Something Borrowed, Something Blue," 1099.
123. Teles, *The Rise of the Conservative Legal Movement*, 277.

CHAPTER 3

1. Kalman, *Legal Realism at Yale, 1927-1960*, 229.
2. *See e.g.* Cass Sunstein, "Constitutionalism after the New Deal," *Harvard Law Review* 101 (1987): 421-510; Bruce Ackerman, *We the People: Transformations* (Cambridge, MA: Harvard University Press, 1998); Stephen Griffin, *American Constitutionalism* (Princeton: Princeton University Press, 1998).
3. *See for example* Sundquist, *Dynamics of the Party System*; MacKuen, Erikson, and Stimson, "Macropartisanship," Green, Palmquist, and Schickler, *Partisan Hearts and Minds*.
4. Sundquist, *Dynamics of the Party System*, 269.
5. *See e.g.* Everett Carll Ladd and Charles Hadley, eds., *Transformations of the American Party System: Political Coalitions from the New Deal to the 1970s* (New York: W.W. Norton & Company, 1975); Kristi Andersen, *The Creation of a Democratic Majority: 1928-1936* (Chicago: University of Chicago Press, 1979); Sidney Milkis and Jerome Mileur, eds., *The New Deal and the Triumph of Liberalism* (Amherst: University of Massachusetts Press, 2002).
6. *See e.g.* Thomas Wolf, William Pederson, and Byron Daynes, eds., *Franklin D. Roosevelt and Congress: The New Deal and Its Aftermath* (New York: M.E. Sharpe, Inc., 2001); Susan Dunn, *Roosevelt's Purge: How F.D.R. Fought to Change the Democratic Party* (Cambridge, MA: Belknap Press, 2012); Jacob Neiheisel, "An Incomplete Failure: The Roosevelt 'Purge' and Mass Support for Responsible Party Government" (Paper presented at the annual meeting of the Western Political Science Association, Portland, OR, March 22-24, 2012).
7. *See e.g.* James Patterson, *Congressional Conservatism and the New Deal: The Growth of the Conservative Coalition in Congress, 1933-1939* (Lexington: University of Kentucky Press, 1967); John Manley, "The Conservative Coalition in Congress," *American Behavioral Scientist* 17 (1973): 223-47; Mack Shelley, *The Permanent Majority: The Conservative Coalition in the United States Congress* (Tuscaloosa: University of Alabama Press, 1983).
8. Sidney Milkis and Jerome Mileur, eds., *The Great Society and the High Tide of Liberalism* (Amherst: University of Massachusetts Press, 2005).
9. *See e.g.* Earl Black and Merle Black, *Politics and Society in the South*; Earl Black and Merle Black, *The Rise of Southern Republicans*; Glenn Feldman,

Painting Dixie Red: When, Where, Why, and How the South Became Republican (Gainesville: University Press of Florida, 2011).

10. *See e.g.* Gilmore, *The Ages of American Law*; Horwitz, *The Transformation of American Law 1870-1960*; Wiecek, *The Lost World of Classical Legal Thought*.
11. *See for example* Kalman, *Legal Realism at Yale, 1927-1960*, 11-13; Singer, "Legal Realism Now," 477-82; William LaPiana, *Logic and Experience: The Origin of Modern American Legal Education* (Oxford: Oxford University Press, 1994), 29-78.
12. Kalman, *Legal Realism at Yale, 1927-1960*, 13.
13. Ibid., 14.
14. Horwitz, *The Transformation of American Law 1870-1960*, 170.
15. Oliver Wendell Holmes, *The Common Law* (Boston: Little, Brown & Company, 1881), 1; Oliver Wendell Holmes, "The Path of the Law," *Harvard Law Review* 10 (1897): 457-78.
16. Roscoe Pound, "Mechanical Jurisprudence," *Columbia Law Review* 8 (1908): 605-23, 605; Roscoe Pound, "Liberty of Contract," *Yale Law Journal* 18 (1909): 454-87, 464.
17. Joseph Bingham, "What is the Law?" *Michigan Law Review* 11 (1912): 1-25, 3.
18. Horwitz, *The Transformation of American Law 1870-1960*, 209.
19. *See for example* Kalman, *Legal Realism at Yale, 1927-1960*, 46; Horwitz, *The Transformation of American Law 1870-1960*, 170; Ronen Shamir, *Managing Legal Uncertainty: Elite Lawyers in the New Deal* (Durham: Duke University Press, 1995), 146.
20. White, "From Sociological Jurisprudence to Realism," 999.
21. Julius Stone, "Roscoe Pound and Sociological Jurisprudence," *Harvard Law Review* 78 (1965): 1578-84, 1581.
22. *See e.g.* Walker Lowry, "Mr. Justice Holmes: The Community vs. the Individual," *California Law Review* 36 (1948): 390-404; Jan Vetter, "The Evolution of Holmes, Holmes and Evolution." *California Law Review* 72 (1984): 343-368; G. Edward White, "Looking at Holmes in the Mirror," *Law & History Review* 4 (1986): 439-65.
23. Edwin Patterson, "Roscoe Pound on Jurisprudence," *Columbia Law Review* 60 (1960): 1124-32, 1130.
24. *See e.g.* John Buenker, John Burnham, and Robert Crunden, *Progressivism* (Cambridge, MA: Schenkman Publishing Company, 1977); Lewis Gould, *America in the Progressive Era, 1890-1914* (New York: Longman, 2001); Michael McGerr, *A Fierce Discontent: The Rise and Fall of the Progressive*

Movement in America, 1870-1920 (Oxford: Oxford University Press., 2003).

25. Gillman, *The Constitution Besieged*, 151.
26. Ibid.
27. Ibid., 8.
28. Westin, "The Supreme Court, the Populist Movement, and the Campaign of 1896," 30.
29. Herbert Croly, *Progressive Democracy* (New York: The Macmillan Company, 1915); Walter Weyl, *The New Democracy: An Essay on Certain Political and Economic Tendencies in the United States* (New York: The Macmillan Company, 1912).
30. *See* David Levy, *Herbert Croly of the New Republic: The Life and Thought of an American Progressive* (Princeton: Princeton University Press, 1985).
31. Kersch, *Constructing Civil Liberties*, 29.
32. Kalman, *Legal Realism at Yale, 1927-1960*, 15.
33. Gail Hupper, "The Rise of an Academic Doctorate in Law: Origins through World War II," *American Journal of Legal History* 49 (2007): 1-60.
34. Ibid., 4.
35. Grant Gilmore, "Legal Realism: Its Cause and Cure," *Yale Law Journal* 70 (1961): 1037-48.
36. LaPiana, *Logic and Experience*, 168.
37. James Herget and Stephen Wallace, "The German Free Law Movement as the Source of American Legal Realism," *Virginia Law Review* 73 (1987): 399-455, 431.
38. Herman Oliphant, "A Return to Stare Decisis," *American Bar Association Journal* 14 (1928): 71-159.
39. Joseph Hutcheson, "The Judgment Intuitive: The Function of the 'Hunch' in Judicial Decision," *Cornell Law Quarterly* 14 (1929): 274-88, 285, 288.
40. Singer, "Legal Realism Now," 481.
41. White, "From Sociological Jurisprudence to Realism," 1017.
42. Samuel Hendel, *Charles Evans Hughes and the Supreme Court* (New York: Russell & Russell, 1951), 78.
43. Ibid., 80, 81.
44. Ibid., 83, 85.
45. Kevin McMahon, *Reconsidering Roosevelt on Race: How the Presidency Paved the Road to Brown* (Chicago: University of Chicago Press, 2003), 28.
46. William Ross, *The Chief Justiceship of Charles Evans Hughes, 1930-1941* (Columbia: University of South Carolina Press, 2007), 17.

47. Sundquist, *Dynamics of the Party System*, 202.
48. "Cardozo Is Named to Supreme Court," *New York Times*, February 16, 1932.
49. Andrew Kaufman, *Cardozo* (Cambridge, MA: Harvard University Press, 1998), 465.
50. Benjamin Cardozo, *The Nature of the Judicial Process* (New Haven: Yale University Press, 1921).
51. *See for example* Gilmore, *The Ages of American Law*, 74-78; Horwitz, *The Transformation of American Law 1870-1960*, 189-92; Kaufman, *Cardozo*, 199-226.
52. Kalman, *Legal Realism at Yale, 1927-1960*, 68.
53. Ibid., 69.
54. Ibid., 74.
55. Ibid., 49.
56. Ibid., 52.
57. Ibid., 45-66.
58. Shamir, *Managing Legal Uncertainty*, 212.
59. Teles, *The Rise of the Conservative Legal Movement*, 28.
60. Ibid.
61. Shamir, *Managing Legal Uncertainty*, 133.
62. Ronen Shamir, "Professionalism and Monopoly of Expertise: Lawyers and Administrative Law, 1933-1937," *Law & Society Review* 27 (1993): 361-98, 389.
63. Shamir, *Managing Legal Uncertainty*, 4.
64. *See for example* Terence Halliday, "Politics and Civic Professionalism: Legal Elites and Cause Lawyers," *Law & Social Inquiry* 24 (1999): 1013-60.
65. LaPiana, *Logic and Experience*, 136.
66. McMahon, *Reconsidering Roosevelt on Race*, 27.
67. Ibid.
68. Whittington, *Political Foundations of Judicial Supremacy*, 56.
69. Clayton, *The Politics of Justice*, 97.
70. Donald Roper, Review of *The New Deal Lawyers* by Peter Irons, *Political Science Quarterly* 98 (1983): 308-9.
71. *See* Peter Irons, *The New Deal Lawyers* (Princeton: Princeton University Press, 1982).
72. Kalman, *Legal Realism at Yale, 1927-1960*, 130-31.

73. William Leuchtenburg, *The Supreme Court Reborn: The Constitutional Revolution in the Age of Roosevelt* (Oxford: Oxford University Press, 1995), 84.
74. Marian McKenna, *Franklin Roosevelt and the Great Constitutional War: The Court-Packing Crisis of 1937* (New York: Fordham University Press, 2002), 153-68.
75. Clayton, *The Politics of Justice*, 124.
76. McKenna, *Franklin Roosevelt and the Great Constitutional War*, 114; McMahon, *Reconsidering Roosevelt on Race*, 70, 71.
77. Shamir, *Managing Legal Uncertainty*, 73.
78. Thurman Arnold, "The Restatement of the Law of Trusts," *Columbia Law Review* 31 (1931): 800-23, 803, 800, 803; Felix Cohen, "Transcendental Nonsense and the Functional Approach," *Columbia Law Review* 35 (1935): 809-49, 809.
79. Karl Llewellyn, "The Constitution as an Institution," *Columbia Law Review* 34 (1934): 1-40, 1, 2; Max Lerner, "Constitution and Court as Symbols," *Yale Law Journal* 46 (1937): 1290-1319, 1298.
80. Hessel Yntema, Review of *A Selection of Cases on the Conflict of Laws* by Joseph Henry Beale, *Columbia Law Review* 28 (1928): 673-75, 675, 674, 675.
81. Robert Swaine, Review of *Cases and Materials on the Law of Corporate Reorganization* by William Douglas and Carrol Shanks, *Columbia Law Review* 32 (1932): 402-3, 402.
82. John Dickinson, "The Law behind Law," *Columbia Law Review* 29 (1929): 113-46, 140; John Dickinson, "The Law behind Law: II," *Columbia Law Review* 29 (1929): 285-319, 314.
83. Mortimer Adler, "Legal Certainty," *Columbia Law Review* 31 (1931): 91-108, 105.
84. Roscoe Pound, "The Future of Law," *Yale Law Journal* 47 (1937): 1-13, 1.
85. Kalman, *Legal Realism at Yale, 1927-1960*, 45.
86. Roscoe Pound, "The Call for a Realist Jurisprudence," *Harvard Law Review* 44 (1931): 697-711, 707.
87. Hermann Kantorowicz, "Some Rationalism about Realism," *Yale Law Journal* 43 (1934): 1240-53, 1247.
88. Joseph Beale, John Laughlin, Randolph Guthrie, and Daniel Sandomire, "Marriage and the Domicil," *Harvard Law Review* 44 (1931): 501-29, 501, 502.
89. Brian Tamanaha, *Beyond the Formalist-Realist Divide: The Role of Politics in Judging* (Princeton: Princeton University Press, 2010), 106.

90. David Rabban, *Law's History: American Legal Thought and the Transatlantic Turn to History* (Cambridge: Cambridge University Press); Ronald Dworkin, "Pragmatism, Rights Answers, and True Banality," in Michael Brint and William Weaver, eds., *Pragmatism in Law and Society* (Boulder, CO: Westview Press, 1991), 368; Kalman, *Legal Realism at Yale, 1927-1960*, 229-31.
91. Cardozo, *The Nature of the Judicial Process*, 115, 55.
92. Horwitz, *The Transformation of American Law 1870-1960*, 192.
93. Ibid., 175.
94. Learned Hand, Review of *The Nature of the Judicial Process* by Benjamin Cardozo, *Harvard Law Review* 35 (1922): 479-81, 480.
95. Cardozo, *The Nature of the Judicial Process*, 116.
96. Rousseau Burch, Review of *The Nature of the Judicial Process* by Benjamin Cardozo, *Yale Law Journal* 31 (1922): 677-81, 681.
97. Jerome Frank, *Law and the Modern Mind* (New York: Brentano's, 1930), 19; Horwitz, *The Transformation of American Law 1870-1960*, 179, 177.
98. Llewellyn, "Legal Illusion," 82.
99. Oscar Cox, Review of *Law and the Modern Mind* by Jerome Frank, *Yale Law Journal* 40 (1931): 670-72, 671, 672.
100. Henry Rottschaefer, Review of *Law and the Modern Mind* by Jerome Frank, *Harvard Law Review* 44 (1931): 481-84, 484.
101. Horwitz, *The Transformation of American Law 1870-1960*, 176.
102. Jerome Frank, Review of *The Bramble Bush: Some Lectures on Law and Its Study* by Karl Llewellyn, *Yale Law Journal* 40 (1931): 1120-25, 1120; Arthur Corbin, Review of *The Bramble Bush: Some Lectures on Law and Its Study* by Karl Llewellyn, *Columbia Law Review* 31 (1931): 515-16, 515.
103. Lawrence Tribe, *God Save This Honorable Court: How the Choice of Supreme Court Justices Shapes Our History* (New York: Random House, 1985), 69.
104. *See* McMahon, *Reconsidering Roosevelt on Race*, 144-76.
105. *See e.g.* H.N. Hirsch, *The Enigma of Felix Frankfurter* (New York: Basic Books, 1981); James Simon, *The Antagonists: Hugo Black, Felix Frankfurter, and Civil Liberties in Modern America* (New York: Simon & Schuster, 1989); Noah Feldman, *Scorpions: The Battles and Triumphs of F.D.R.'s Great Supreme Court Justices* (New York: Twelve Publishing, 2010).
106. Keck, *The Most Activist Supreme Court in History*, 41.
107. *Colegrove v. Green*, 328 U.S. 549, 556 (1946).
108. Urofsky, "Conflict among the Brethren," 81-82.

109. Keck, *The Most Activist Supreme Court in History*, 29.
110. *Palko v. Connecticut*, 302 U.S. 319, 325 (1937).
111. Robert Peck, "New Supreme Court Justices and the 'Freshman Effect,'" *Charleston Law Review* 4 (2009): 149-70, 161.
112. Merle Miller, *Plain Speaking: An Oral Biography of Harry S. Truman* (New York: Berkley Publishing Companies, 1974), 243.
113. Kalman, *Legal Realism at Yale, 1927-1960*, 43.
114. *See e.g.* Urofsky, "Conflict among the Brethren;" Melvin Urofsky, *Division and Discord: The Supreme Court under Stone and Vinson, 1941-1953* (Columbia: University of South Carolina Press, 1997); Bruce Murphy, *Wild Bill: The Legend and Life of Bill Douglas* (New York: Random House, 2003).
115. Stephen Presser, Review of *To Secure These Rights: The Declaration of Independence and Constitutional Interpretation* by Scott Douglas Gerber, *Constitutional Commentary* 14 (1997): 229-30, 229.
116. David Nichols, *A Matter of Justice: Eisenhower and the Beginning of the Civil Rights Revolution* (New York: Simon & Schuster, 2007), 91; Kim Isaac Eisler, *A Justice for All: William J. Brennan, Jr. and the Decisions that Transformed America* (New York: Simon & Schuster, 1993), 89.

CHAPTER 4

1. Gillman, *The Constitution Besieged*, 3.
2. Wiecek, *The Lost World of Classical Legal Thought*, 3.
3. *See e.g.* Walter Dean Burnham, "The System of 1896: An Analysis," in Paul Kleppner, et al., *The Evolution of American Electoral Systems* (Westport, CT: Greenwood Press, 1983); Sundquist, *Dynamics of the Party System*; Paul Kleppner, *Continuity and Change in Electoral Politics, 1893-1928* (Westport, CT: Greenwood Press, 1987).
4. Sundquist, *Dynamics of the Party System*, 154.
5. Ibid., 164.
6. *See e.g.* Scott Roger, "Uncle Joe Cannon: The Brakeman of the House of Representatives, 1903-1911," in Roger Davidson, Susan Webb Hammond, and Raymond Smock, eds., *Masters of the House: Congressional Leadership Over Two Centuries* (Boulder, CO: Westview Press, 1998); Steven Smith and Gerald Gamm, "The Dynamics of Party Government in Congress," in Lawrence Dodd and Bruce Oppenheimer, eds., *Congress Reconsidered* (Washington: C.Q. Press, 2013).

7. Garland Tucker, *The High Tide of American Conservatism: Davis, Coolidge, and the 1924 Election* (Austin, TX: Emerald Book Company, 2010).
8. Sundquist, *Dynamics of the Party System*, 196.
9. Michael Phillips, *The Lochner Court, Myth and Reality: Substantive Due Process from the 1890s to the 1930s* (Westport, CT: Praeger Publishers, 2001), 32.
10. Wiecek, *The Lost World of Classical Legal Thought*, 126-33.
11. David Barnum, "Lochner Revisited and Reappraised," *Review of Politics* 55 (1993): 533-35, 534.
12. Eric Foner, "Abolitionism and the Labor Movement in Antebellum America," in Eric Foner, ed., *Politics and Ideology in the Age of the Civil War* (Oxford: Oxford University Press, 1980), 73.
13. Gillman, *The Constitution Besieged*, 15.
14. Francis Hilliard, *The Law of Torts* (Boston: Little, Brown & Company, 1859), vii; *See also* Novak, *The People's Welfare*.
15. Horwitz, *The Transformation of American Law 1870-1960*, 13.
16. Novak, *The People's Welfare*, 19-50.
17. Ibid., 2; *The Slaughterhouse Cases*, 83 U.S. 36, 62 (1873).
18. Horwitz, *The Transformation of American Law 1780-1860*, 255.
19. Ibid., 25, 24.
20. Boorstin, *The Americans*, 35.
21. Wiecek, *The Lost World of Classical Legal Thought*, 68.
22. Horwitz, *The Transformation of American Law 1870-1960*, 9.
23. Ibid., 11.
24. *See for example* Louis Menand, *The Metaphysical Club* (New York: Farrar, Straus & Giroux, 2001), 226, 274.
25. Horwitz, *The Transformation of American Law 1870-1960*, 16.
26. Christopher Columbus Langdell, *A Selection of Cases on the Law of Contracts* (Boston: Little, Brown & Company, 1871), vi.
27. Wiecek, *The Lost World of Classical Legal Thought*, 93.
28. Robert Gordon, "The Case For (and Against) Harvard," *Michigan Law Review* 93 (1995): 1231-60, 1235.
29. Joel Seligman, *The High Citadel: The Influence of Harvard Law School* (Boston: Houghton Mifflin Company, 1978), 32-42.
30. *See e.g.* Gillman, *The Constitution Besieged*; Wiecek, *The Lost World of Classical Legal Thought*; David Bernstein, *Rehabilitating Lochner: Defending Individual Rights against Progressive Reform* (Chicago: University of Chicago Press, 2011).

31. Wiecek, *The Lost World of Classical Legal Thought*, 127.
32. Ibid., 126-33.
33. *Munn v. Illinois*, 94 U.S. 113, 134 (1877).
34. Westin, "The Supreme Court, the Populist Movement, and the Campaign of 1896," 20, 19.
35. Wiecek, *The Lost World of Classical Legal Thought*, 86.
36. Ibid., 134.
37. *See for example* Tim McNeese, *The Robber Barons and the Sherman Anti-Trust Act: Reshaping American Business* (New York: Chelsea House Publishers, 2008), 90.
38. *Pollock v. Farmers' Loan & Trust Company*, 157 U.S. 429, 583 (1895); Westin, "The Supreme Court, the Populist Movement, and the Campaign of 1896," 23.
39. John Schmidhauser, *Constitutional Law in American Politics* (Monterey, CA: Brooks/Cole Publishing Company, 1984), 264.
40. Ibid., 258.
41. Walter Dean Burnham, "Constitutional Moments and Punctuated Equilibria: A Political Scientist Confronts Bruce Ackerman's We the People," *Yale Law Journal* 108 (1999): 2237-77, 2256.
42. Gilmore, *The Ages of American Law*, 68.
43. Wiecek, *The Lost World of Classical Legal Thought*, 74.
44. Rendigs Fels, "The Long-Wave Depression, 1873-97," *Review of Economics and Statistics* 31 (1949): 69-73, 69.
45. Jeremy Brecher, *Strike!* (Boston: South End Press, 1999), 40.
46. Wiecek, *The Lost World of Classical Legal Thought*, 84.
47. John Dillon, "Property—Its Rights and Duties in Our Legal and Social Systems," *American Law Review* 29 (1895): 161-88, 161; Christopher Tiedeman, *A Treatise on the Limitations of Police Power in the United States* (St. Louis: F.H. Thomas Law Book Company, 1886), vi.
48. Wiecek, *The Lost World of Classical Legal Thought*, 86, 85.
49. Ibid., 94.
50. Seligman, *The High Citadel*, 41.
51. *See for example* Allan Nevins, *Grover Cleveland: A Study in Courage* (New York: Dodd, Mead & Company, 1932), 613; H.P. Jeffers, *An Honest President: The Life and Presidencies of Grover Cleveland* (New York: William Morrow & Company, 2000), 305-6; Henry Graff, *Grover Cleveland* (New York: Times Books, 2002), 129.
52. *See for example* Richard Franklin Bensel, *The Political Economy of American Industrialization, 1877-1900* (Cambridge: Cambridge University

Press, 2000), 344-46; Andrew Polsky, "The Political Economy of Partisan Regimes: Lessons from Two Republican Eras," *Polity* 35 (2003): 595-612, 602.

53. Schmidhauser, *Constitutional Law in American Politics*, 255.
54. Owen Fiss, *Troubled Beginnings of the Modern State, 1888-1910* (New York: Macmillan Publishers, 1993), 39.
55. *See e.g.* Lawrence Goodwyn, *The Populist Movement: A Short History of the Agrarian Revolt in America* (Oxford: Oxford University Press, 1978); Michael Kazin, *The Populist Persuasion: An American History* (Ithaca, NY: Cornell University Press, 1995); Charles Postel, *The Populist Vision* (Oxford: Oxford University Press, 2007).
56. Westin, "The Supreme Court, the Populist Movement, and the Campaign of 1896," 31.
57. Gerard Magliocca, "Constitutional False Positives and the Populist Moment," *Notre Dame Law Review* 81 (2006): 821-88, 879.
58. Westin, "The Supreme Court, the Populist Movement, and the Campaign of 1896," 34.
59. Ibid., 33.
60. Sundquist, *Dynamics of the Party System*, 169.
61. Ibid.
62. Ibid., 166.
63. Ibid., 175-76.
64. Hollis Bailey, "Situs of Choses in Action," *Harvard Law Review* 11 (1897): 95-113, 95; Christopher Tiedeman, "Methods of Legal Education," *Yale Law Journal* 1 (1892): 150-58, 154.
65. James Hayden, "The 'Eight-Hour Law,'" *Yale Law Journal* 2 (1893): 197-205, 201.
66. Frederic Foster, "The Doctrine of the United States Supreme Court of Property Affected by a Public Interest and Its Tendencies," *Yale Law Journal* 5 (1895): 49-82, 57; George Yeaman, "Legislation and Individual Action," *Yale Law Journal* 2 (1893): 173-80, 174.
67. Oliver Wendell Holmes, "Law in Science and Science in Law," *Harvard Law Review* 12 (1899): 443-63, 452; Isaac Franklin Russell, "The Most Ancient Law," *Yale Law Journal* 7 (1898): 377-84, 378.
68. Jeremiah Smith, "The Use of Maxims in Jurisprudence," *Harvard Law Review* 9 (1895): 13-26, 24.
69. Arthur Hadley, "The Relation between Economics and Politics," *Yale Law Journal* 8 (1899): 194-206, 202; Edward Whitney, "Constitutional

Questions under the Federal Anti-Trust Law," *Yale Law Journal* 7 (1898): 285-94, 294.

70. Bernstein, *Rehabilitating Lochner*, 20.
71. Magliocca, "Constitutional False Positives and the Populist Moment," 845.
72. Burnham, "Constitutional Moments and Punctuated Equilibria," 2256.
73. Magliocca, "Constitutional False Positives and the Populist Moment," 821; Ackerman, *We the People*, 187.
74. Ibid., 885.
75. *See e.g.* Hendel, *Charles Evans Hughes and the Supreme Court*; Robert Wesser, *Charles Evans Hughes: Politics and Reform in New York, 1905-1910* (Ithaca, NY: Cornell University Press, 1967); Ross, *The Chief Justiceship of Charles Evans Hughes, 1930-1941*.
76. *Chicago, Burlington & Quincy Railroad Company v. McGuire*, 219 U.S. 549, 570 (1911).
77. *Houston, East & West Texas Railway Company v. United States*, 234 U.S. 342, 351.
78. *See for example* Richard Friedman, "Tribal Myths: Ideology and the Confirmation of Supreme Court Nominations," *Yale Law Journal* 95 (1986): 1283-1320; James Bond, *I Dissent: The Legacy of Chief Justice James Clark McReynolds* (Fairfax, VA: George Mason University Press, 1992).
79. Friedman, "Tribal Myths," 1299.
80. Gerald Dunne, *Hugo Black and the Judicial Revolution* (New York: Simon & Schuster, 1977), 78; Howard Ball, *Hugo L. Black: Cold Steel Warrior* (Oxford: Oxford University Press, 2006), 89.
81. *See e.g.* Barry Cushman, "Rethinking the New Deal Court," *Virginia Law Review* 80 (1994): 201-61; Richard Friedman, "Switching Time and Other Thought Experiments: The Hughes Court and Constitutional Transformation," *University of Pennsylvania Law Review* 142 (1994): 1891-1984; James Henretta, "Charles Evans Hughes and the Strange Death of Liberal America," *Law & History Review* 24 (2006): 115-71.
82. *See for example* G. Edward White, *The Constitution and the New Deal* (Cambridge, MA: Harvard University Press, 2000), 81.
83. Miriam Galston, "Activism and Restraint: The Evolution of Harlan Fiske Stone's Judicial Philosophy," *Tulane Law Review* 70 (1995): 137-86, 144.
84. Ibid.
85. Kalman, *Legal Realism at Yale, 1927-1960*, 69.
86. Galston, "Activism and Restraint," 146-49.

87. Peter Fish, "Spite Nominations to the United States Supreme Court: Herbert C. Hoover, Owen J. Roberts, and the Politics of Presidential Vengeance in Retrospect," *Kentucky Law Journal* 77 (1989): 545-76, 561, 545.
88. *See e.g.* John Semonche, *Charting the Future: The Supreme Court Responds to a Changing Society, 1890-1920* (Westport, CT: Greenwood Press, 1978); Melvin Urofsky, "State Courts and Protective Legislation during the Progressive Era: A Reevaluation," *Journal of American History* 72 (1985): 63-91; Brian Tamanaha, "Understanding Legal Realism," *Texas Law Review* 87 (2009): 731-85.
89. Tamanaha, *Beyond the Formalist-Realist Divide*, 99.
90. *See e.g.* Munroe Smith, "The Development of American Constitutional Law," *Proceedings of the Academy of Political Science* 3 (1913): 52-69; Charles Warren, "The Progressiveness of the United States Supreme Court," *Columbia Law Review* 13 (1913): 294-313.
91. Phillips, *The Lochner Court, Myth and Reality*, 56.

CHAPTER 5

1. Teles, *The Rise of the Conservative Legal Movement*, 23.
2. Holmes, *The Common Law*, 1.
3. *See e.g.* John Judis, "America the Liberal," *The New Republic*, November 5, 2008; Harold Meyerson, "A Real Realignment," *Washington Post*, November 7, 2008; Jonathan Chait, "Has the Emerging Democratic Majority Emerged?" *New York Magazine*, November 14, 2012.
4. *See e.g.* Gerald Seib, "U.S. Shifted Party, Not Ideology," *The Wall Street Journal*, January 19, 2010; David Crockett, "Candidate Obama and the Dilemmas of Political Time," *The Forum* 9 (2011): 1-22; Jack Balkin, "What It Will Take for Barack Obama to Become the Next F.D.R.," *The Atlantic*, November 1, 2012.
5. *See e.g.* Mark Graber, "A Tale Told by a President," *Yale Law & Policy Review* 28 (2010): 13-25; Andrew Cohen, "For Barack Obama, Law Professor, the Time to Lecture Is Now," *The Atlantic*, April 4, 2012; John Yoo, "On Judicial Review—President Obama Seems to Understand It Poorly," *National Review*, April 24, 2012.
6. Yoo, "On Judicial Review."
7. Josh Gerstein, "Obama's Search for 'Empathy' Shapes Supreme Court Replacement Debate," *Politico*, May 4, 2009.
8. Nancy Maveety, "A Transformative Politics of Judicial Selection? President Obama and the Federal Judiciary," in Steven Schier, ed.,

Transforming America: Barack Obama in the White House (Lanham, MD: Rowman & Littlefield Publishers, 2011), 173.

9. Justin Crowe and Christopher Karpowitz, "Where Have You Gone, Sherman Minton? The Decline of the Short-Term Supreme Court Justice," *Perspectives on Politics* 5 (2007): 425-45.
10. Skowronek, *The Politics Presidents Make*, 407, 31.
11. *See* Gerald Rosenberg, *The Hollow Hope: Can Courts Bring About Social Change?* (Chicago: University of Chicago Press, 1991).

Cases Cited

Adair v. United States, 208 U.S. 161 (1908)
Adkins v. Children's Hospital, 261 U.S. 525 (1923)
Allgeyer v. Louisiana, 165 U.S. 578 (1897)
Brown v. Board of Education of Topeka, 347 U.S. 483 (1954)
Chicago, Burlington & Quincy Railroad Company v. McGuire, 219 U.S. 549 (1911)
Chicago, Milwaukee & St. Paul Railway Company v. Minnesota, 134 U.S. 418 (1890)
Citizens United v. Federal Election Commission, 558 U.S. 310 (2010)
Colegrove v. Green, 328 U.S. 549 (1946)
Coppage v. Kansas, 236 U.S. 1 (1915)
Dennis v. United States, 341 U.S. 494 (1951)
Dickerson v. United States, 530 U.S. 428 (2000)
District of Columbia v. Heller, 554 U.S. 570 (2008)
Dred Scott v. Sandford, 60 U.S. 393 (1857)
Gaines v. Canada, 305 U.S. 337 (1938)
Gideon v. Wainwright, 372 U.S. 335 (1963)
Hammer v. Dagenhart, 247 U.S. 251 (1918)
Houston, East & West Texas Railway Company v. United States, 234 U.S. 342 (1914)
In re Debs, 158 U.S. 564 (1895)
In re Jacobs, 98 N.Y. 98 (1885)
Lochner v. New York, 198 U.S. 45 (1905)
McLaurin v. Oklahoma State Regents, 339 U.S. 637 (1950)
Minersville School District v. Gobitis, 310 U.S. 586 (1940)
Miranda v. Arizona, 384 U.S. 436 (1966)
Muller v. Oregon, 208 U.S. 412 (1908)
Munn v. Illinois, 94 U.S. 113 (1877)
Nebbia v. New York, 291 U.S. 502 (1934)
Palko v. Connecticut, 302 U.S. 319 (1937)
Pollock v. Farmers' Loan & Trust Company, 157 U.S. 429 (1895)
Regents of the University of California v. Bakke, 438 U.S. 265 (1978)
Roe v. Wade, 410 U.S. 113 (1973)
Smith v. Allwright, 321 U.S. 649 (1944)
Springer v. United States, 102 U.S. 586 (1881)
Sweatt v. Painter, 339 U.S. 629 (1950)

The Employers' Liability Cases, 207 U.S. 463 (1908)
The Slaughterhouse Cases, 83 U.S. 36 (1873)
Thornburgh v. American College of Obstetricians and Gynecologists, 476 U.S. 747 (1986)
United Mine Workers of America v. Red Jacket Consolidated Coal & Coke Company, 275 U.S. 536 (1927)
United States v. Carolene Products Company, 304 U.S. 144 (1938)
United States v. Darby, 312 U.S. 100 (1941)
United States v. E.C. Knight Company, 156 U.S. 1 (1895)
United States v. Lopez, 514 U.S. 549 (1995)
West Coast Hotel Company v. Parrish, 300 U.S. 379 (1937)
Wickard v. Filburn, 317 U.S. 111 (1942)

Index